Contents

BECOMING CHRISTIAN

Becoming Christian

by
Alexander Ganoczy

Translated by
John G. Lynch, C.S.P.

PAULIST PRESS
New York / Ramsey / Toronto

A Paulist Press edition, originally published under the title *Devenir Chrétien,* Les Editions du Cerf, Paris, France, 1973.

Library of Congress
Catalog Card Number: 76-23530

ISBN: 0-8091-1980-3

Published by Paulist Press
Editorial Office: 1865 Broadway, N.Y., N.Y. 10023
Business Office: 545 Island Road, Ramsey, N.J. 07446

Printed and bound in the
United States of America

Translator's Preface

I first met Alexander Ganoczy in 1966 in Paris, where he helped direct my doctoral studies in infant baptism at the Institut Catholique de Paris. I remember him as a quiet, serious scholar, with an amazing breadth of insight. Many of the questions we discussed then are presented in this study; now, as then, he was especially attuned to "historicity" in doing theology.

"Historicity" is really the key to understanding Ganoczy's thought in this study on baptism. Constantly searching for what is most authentic in our Christian heritage, he examines scriptural and patristic evidence concerning the sacrament, careful to sort out those witnesses faithful to an historical understanding of Christian existence. He criticizes many of the Church Fathers for their non-historical approach to the sacrament. Baptism, he insists must be the beginning of a journey, or it is no sacrament at all.

There is no room for magical illumination or instant salvation in Ganoczy's thought. Christian life is a pilgrimage in freedom. In moving from the past through the present to create the future, the baptized enter into solidarity with Jesus, sharing his destiny and espousing his life as their own. Their lives marked by the cross and the resurrection, Christians live in hope, straining to go beyond what is to what will be.

In this pilgrimage, Christians live sensitive to their temporal and relational worlds. Their past history, they know, gives direction and character to their future. The future, in turn, gives light, possibility, and hope to the past. In their relationships, Christians taste the dialectic between freedom and slavery, experiencing the tension inevitable in walking in "newness of life."

Ganoczy, beginning with these contemporary notions of temporal and relational historicity, appeals to Mounier's personalism and contemporary neo-Marxism as valuable resources in unraveling the complex variety of witnesses to baptism in the New Testament and the Fathers of the Church. He weaves together Mounier's emphasis on personal encounter and the neo-Marxist stress on hope to build up a provocative and intelligent theology of the sacrament.

Such a challenging adventure is not without its dangers and weaknesses. L. Renwart, reviewing Ganoczy's study in the prestigious *Nouvelle Revue Théologique,* finds the author's treatment of original sin inadequate. Ganoczy, not really attempting an over-all synthesis of the problem, does criticize Augustine's theory of original sin as profoundly non-historical. Even though Renwart's observation is true, Ganoczy's succinct insights into a contemporary understanding of original sin remain valid. Renwart feels, too, that the author does not give proper emphasis to the role of God's free gift of love in the whole question of human freedom. Again, although Renwart's observation has merit, Ganoczy's concern that the Church—and parents —act with historically responsible freedom in baptizing remains crucial and correct.

In his treatment of contemporary pastoral problems Ganoczy does not pretend to be exhaustively thorough. This is a book for raising intelligent questions and offering important perspectives on baptism and its related pastoral issues. The author insists that there can be no understanding of the sacrament apart from history. Baptism, he writes, is the sacrament of Christian progress and hope. The baptized are called to "absorb in their reflections and encounters all the diverse factions they encounter, living them out in tension and in tears, to build up the Kingdom of God under the sign of their risen Lord's cross."

I am indebted to Father Kevin Lynch, C.S.P. of the Paulist Press, to Anna Martha Donohoe, and to Sister Jeannette Normandin for their encouragement and assistance in preparing this translation. It is written for Christopher, whom I baptized nine years ago.

John G. Lynch, C.S.P., S.T.D.
Washington, D.C.
Spring, 1976

Foreword

The purpose of this study is not simply to reformulate the Catholic doctrine of baptism and grace. I do not intend to enter into the debate for or against infant baptism, be that on the level of dogma, liturgy, or pastoral practice. My goal is to spell out systematically the *anthropological* reality signified and enacted in baptism. With growing unanimity, contemporary theology tends to situate this reality within the *historicity* of human existence and from there to the historicity of Christian existence. Such a fundamentally historical understanding of human existence harmonizes with both biblical thought and two important contemporary philosophical currents: existentialism and Marxism. This harmonizing of approach is extremely useful, so long as one follows each school of thought to its logical conclusions. My intention is to examine Christianity's specific identity in the midst of the other "salvific ways" competing in today's world.

1
The Historicity
of Human Existence

Human beings are historical beings. They exist to the extent that they become, joining both continuity and change in themselves. They can change or remain the same; they are history, and they have their own history.

These packed phrases sum up what I call human historicity. Yet questions still remain: What are the component parts of historicity? Where can it be found? In response to these questions, I propose two areas for consideration: temporal historicity and relational historicity.

I
Temporal Personal Historicity

People live in an ensemble of temporal relationships stemming from their birth, actions, passions, desires, and experiences. Indeed, their very freedom must exist in implicit or explicit dialogue with these situations; time is the place where they exercise their freedom.[1] Once people choose their moments for play, work, and pleasure, they establish themselves as masters of their time. Sometimes, of course, unexpected

things happen in their lives. Events come without their
choosing. They may not like them or find them desira-
ble; still they must live them as moments in their lives.
In this situation, they are no longer time's masters but
its servants. Life's rhythm is dictated to them. Whether
by a factory whistle or a spouse's call, they find themselves called by a multitude of situations they do not directly choose.

These temporal relationships are not mere ac-
cidents impinging upon a person, the changeless substance. Nor are they events peripheral to human beings,
themselves essences elevated to the individual or personal levels. Rather, these relationships constitute a
person's being insofar as he or she is temporal.

From this perspective, I can say "I am the work I
have chosen to do"; "I am the act of injustice in which
I am engaged." I am my choice. I am my act. In choosing and bringing about the moments in my life, I am
those moments. What I accomplish in a particular act
or at a particular moment is myself. I am, therefore,
what I have done, be that sinful or virtuous, loving or
hating.

My past, then, has made me what I am. The time I
have fulfilled has constituted me and, to a certain extent, demolished me. My past is irrevocable. I may
regret my faults and be satisfied with my good deeds,
but in no way can I make them cease to be. My past
remains with me as an object; it is part of the objec-
tified region of who I am. Even though I can in no way
deny my past, I can however change, alter, and even
uproot it.

This objective part of my temporal history has
both a luminous and an obscure face, and I must accept
its ambivalence. Even if I disapprove of certain actions

in my past, I must assume responsibility for them in my plans for the future. They have marked me and I am answerable for them. They enter into the critical dialogue I carry on in the present with myself and with others. Even if I am "converted," I do not reduce my past to ashes. I may want to burn what I once adored (or even adore what I once burned), but the world I once lived remains always with me. It walks with me in all its ambivalence, carrying the mark of my past attachments and refusals. My past remains the point of reference for my present and future freedom, continuing on as the object I must reckon with in every decision

The past I have chosen, then, is part of me; I am that past.

But what of the past that has been imposed upon me? Am I equally my past that I have not chosen? Here, too, the answer is "yes." True, the intensity of such historical objectivity is less. If, for instance, I was entirely in a state of refusal when I was forced to act in a certain way or live out a difficult situation, the weight of that past bears more lightly on me than that of my deliberate actions. But even the imposed past is mine—and irrevocably so, however golden or detestable a prison it forced upon me. To the extent that past time, even in an externally imposed state, was my time, it remains part of the history I am and continues to form me. The proof? That I remember it and recount it as part of my life experience.

The experience of imposed events is as much a component of personal historicity as is free choice. No one is the sovereign elector of his or her own destiny; no one lives in total independence. People also submit to life; they do not simply choose it. In fact, there is a natural conformity built into their very origins. On the biological level, for instance, they are marked and formed by structures outside of their own choosing. Even on the levels of intellect, will, and conscience they are subjected to imposed experience. Experience is not simply choice; it is a composite of events that touch them, whether they like them or not. Experience may enrich or impoverish. Whatever the case, it is part of everyone's existential baggage and cannot be thrown off.

What, though, of all that is forgotten? Does forgetting events from childhood or adolescence deliver a person from them? Depth-psychology and psychoanalysis answer "no." Part of any human being's historicity is the subconscious. Children, for instance, may experience a sudden shock that will have its effect only much later in life. They may have no recollection of what happened; their awareness at the time it occurred may have been clouded or distracted, but it has marked and shaped them and influenced an important aspect of their being. Neither forgetfulness nor lack of full awareness does away with what happened at a particular moment in their history. What happened remains. Human beings have their own decisions and experiences that form their own temporal historicity. To these they can—and must—return when they look to the total picture of their own lives.

In planning the future, for example, these moments already chosen or submitted to are important, since planning and foresight cannot be made apart from the past. Human dignity demands that freedom be exercised at the frontier between the past and the future, for there creativity lies—conscious, responsible, and constructive. Freedom, therefore, must be exercised historically. The future is to be invented, organized, and loved in an historical context. Otherwise temporal historicity loses the salvific dimension the future brings. In creating their future, people become what they are. They move toward what is not yet seen, known, or lived, and thereby free themselves from the influences formed in the past.

But not completely! For in projecting their future, human beings can never ignore or eliminate this past that is so irreversibly and objectively part of their lives. It is there, and nothing in the world can dislodge it. Remaining present with both its friendly and hostile faces, the past serves as the springboard for the future. However different they may be, past and future work together to form human history. The past may seem to be only a dead weight to be cast away. But in reality it is linked to the future, as a root is to a tree. The true radical, for instance, goes to the root of things and rediscovers his origins, thence fashioning anew the voyage another person has already completed. The past nourishes the future.

It can never, however, completely determine the future, since it is not by virtue of a biological, *causal* relationship that a person's past is the root of his or her future; the relationship is one of finality. The past enters the picture in its vitally radical character only insofar as it is illuminated by the terminal point of human life. A person's future destiny brings true meaning to his or her past.

The past, therefore, is the beginning of an accomplishment; as freedom's foundation, it is the starting point for a long journey. Past history has this purpose: it is the foundation for projected choices. But the past does more than simply lay the foundation. Because it is itself made up of choices and experiences received, it gives direction and character to the future. Freedom cannot begin to move without the starting point the past provides. People must lean on their past for their future, and to that extent the past conditions their freedom.

As a starting point, the past can be contradicted or followed; otherwise there would be no freedom. It must first of all be received with its positive and negative implications. In realistically receiving their past, human beings begin to fulfill their calling and enter into their temporal historicity.

All that has been said so far, however abstract and distant it may seem from concrete daily existence, is drawn from man's fundamentally communitarian condition. I have begun with this inquiry into temporal historicity only to lead to a consideration of relational, communitarian historicity.

II
RELATIONAL, COMMUNITARIAN HISTORICITY

Two important trends characterize contemporary anthropology's relational dimension. The first, the personalist, takes as its starting point the affirmation that a person's primordial relationship is the reciprocal I-THOU communication.[2] The Marxist trend claims that a human being is basically a totality of social relationships, the concretization of the very society in which he lives and works.[3] Personalists stress mutual love and mutual understanding as the fundamental factors in human historicity. They propose: "I become what I am by the fact that I receive myself from another and that I give myself to that other." Their priority goes to bilateral relationships, be that on the level of man to man or of man to God.

Orthodox Marxists, on the other hand, emphasize collective solidarity—the action that a sociologically homogeneous group deploys to rise above its alienation toward ever-increasing freedom. For Marxists, the factors of historicity act first from the collective to the individual; the individual simply reacts more or less independently within the collective. But the collective remains the basic "infrastructure" from which the individual can build a "superstructure." Orthodox Marxists will say: "I become what I am from the fact that my social, economic, and cultural conditions (and the collective action flowing from them) integrate me into their movements in a dialectical manner and invite me to commitment."

It is highly significant that neo-Marxists are in the process of renouncing a strictly collective anthropology in favor of uniting a person's social and personal spheres more organically. Lukács, Adorno, Horkheimer, Marcuse, and Garaudy (together with Czechoslovak and Yugoslav neo-Marxists) want to save man from the oppressive and dehumanizing anonymity of collectives, institutions, and social classes.[4] They speak again and again of love, criticism, and personal decision as "sine qua non" conditions for any real promotion of humanity toward its proper fullness, condemning all forms of capitalistic or socialistic totalitarianism. For these thinkers, what counts is no longer Marx's "wahres Wesen" (a person's true essence to be re-established in the classless society); they advocate "dynamic transcendence," by which humanity moves toward a better situation, however imperfect and unfinished it may be. Their key word is more "hope" than "unity."[5]

The Marxist and personalist trends set the horizons for describing relational historicity. "Relational," in this perspective, does not refer only to person-to-person relationships, but to all relationships between individuals and the different groups, communities, and collectives they encounter. It speaks to all social relationships, be they primary (family ties) or secondary (professional or organizational ties). Within these various "relational" arenas human historicity is born. Insofar as people are present to one another or choose to encounter each other, they create history; they activate their becoming. But this activation need not arise from harmonious relationships—here, as with temporal historicity, ambivalence comes into play.

Every presence and every encounter produces both harmony and discord. People do not exist in a "pure state," and neither do encounters among them. The most exalted complete union of love always carries with it a zone of non-compenetration; something is missing, and lovers sense a fuller, yet impossible union. There can never be a reciprocal presence without a corresponding reciprocal absence. The converse is also true. The most consummate lack of unity carries with it some aspects of union: my teeth planted in my enemy's arm, for example, at least unites the biter with the bitten! Brothers often find themselves in a relationship of enmity; and it would be hard to find an individual relational history that did not include some tales of disunity. Anthropologically speaking it is normal and even salutary to have an element of confrontation in every communion. Otherwise, a kind of listless uniformity— harmony with no tales to tell—would paralyze any personal growth. If there were no lived differences or no diversities accepted as such, human beings would fall back to the level of animals, plants, or inanimate things, neither knowing that they are different nor wondering why.

The basic fact of sexual differentiation, together with an awareness of our sexual particularities, indicates how much polarity is constitutive of human existence. Without trying to turn universal human history into a battle of the sexes, it is at least opportune to point out that masculinity and femininity give rise to many tensions. These tensions do find partial resolution in spiritual fecundity and physical sexual union, but they also continue to generate on-going antagonisms. Every type of presence and encounter between persons of different sex, mentality, race, faith, and social class is charged with harmony and discord. Each, in its tension and ambivalence, activates relational historicity.

In relational historicity, the otherness of another person plays a role analogous to the past in temporal historicity. Just as the past forces persons to refer to the reality in them that conditions their future, so another person squarely and unavoidably before them forces acceptance of the relationships in their lives as they are. There is nothing like prolonged encounter, continual presence, or renewed confrontation to discover the truth of another person and at the same time discover one's own capacity to be open to others.

Relational historicity does not put us into contact only with the ambivalence between harmony and discord in our encounters. We also meet two other dialectical poles in our relationships: freedom and slavery. Certainly communities exist that are marked by an open, liberating, creative, atmosphere and wonderfully personalistic friendships. But others are characterized by nothing but alienation, withdrawal, and mutual oppression—what Adorno has called "natural tumors."[6]

In such communities membership is reduced to amorphous anonymity. Even groups of Christians can degenerate into such communities, for the factors of depersonalization are built into every society and every community. It suffices to yield to the forces of inertia affecting every human relationship. Even in love, for instance, the desire to give coincides with the desire to possess, so that together with love's urge to sacrifice for the beloved runs the urge of concupiscence to seize the beloved as an object to be dominated and possessed. Once "eros" is no longer guided by "agape" (disinterested love), or at least by "philia" (friendship love), it degenerates into a grasping, intolerant force. The reverse is also true. "Agape" and "philia" run the risk of becoming angelic, insensitive to the needs of man as a living body, should "eros" be ignored.

What this dialectic between self-gift and possession signifies is verified analogously in every social and communal relationship. To reduce the dialectic so that one of its component parts becomes the sole interpreter of reality leads to an oppressive and dehumanizing picture of humankind. Any kind of ideological monism, reducing pluralities to a single idea, dogma, or philosophy, leads to totalitarianism, where the particular masters the whole. A totalitarian father, for instance, becomes an oppressive enslaving presence for his family. A "monistic" society, centering everything on one class, party, or confessional creed, must necessarily have recourse to oppressive, dehumanizing structures—its police forces or its inquisitions. Even a church that allows only one trend in its dogma or its discipline remains underdeveloped, if not outright oppressive. To avoid such totalitarianism, the dialectic between what is individual and what is pluralistic must remain a major part in any relational historicity, whether individual or communal.

To designate the principle that allows for the creation of communities capable of burgeoning forth without overlooking or suppressing the proper historicity of the individual members, I propose the notion of "communional transcendence." I do not mean "metaphysical transcendence" that was used in the past, for instance, to speak of the difference between a natural and supernatural order of things. Instead, I mean, first of all, a dynamism enabling two or more persons or groups to rise above the limits separating them and enter into some kind of communion with one another. Secondly, once this level of communion is achieved, they can go beyond their newly-found union toward a common future existence. The two steps in this dynamic process need not follow one another in chronological order; they can very well coincide or even work in reverse order, depending on the concrete history of the persons involved.

Every community and every society worthy of the name "historical" must allow for "communional transcendence." They must facilitate valid interpersonal, intersocial, and international relationships, at the same time encouraging these "inter" groups to go beyond themselves. Each community, truly conscious of its relational historicity, becomes by that very awareness a place for freedom, presence, and encounter. Such awareness, of course, does not eliminate diversity, tension, and confrontation. Rather, an aware society gathers its tensions together and orients them toward its own goals and purposes, recognizing that the individual paths to those goals are necessarily variant and diverse.

I could continue this reflection on the two prin-

cipal dimensions of human historicity—the temporal
and the relational—to show now how this anthropological point of view applies to baptism as an historical
process. But I think it is preferable to look again at the
very origins of this point of view to see if its genesis is
so modern and so secular that Christianity must actually move beyond itself to join with it.

III
THE ORIGINS OF THE
HISTORICAL UNDERSTANDING OF HUMANKIND

The origins of our Western historical understanding of humankind lie in the ancient Mediterranean
world. From there ran forth the great currents of
thought that gave rise to Western civilization and its
offspring, the industrial society.

Not all those currents of thought were historical,
as I am using the term in this book. In those ancient
worlds, many eyes were focused first on eternal images.
They looked to ideas and ideals, norms and laws, and
believed them to be immutable. Authority was rooted
in what was ancient, invariable, and firmly rooted to
the ideal. Take, for instance, the Platonic concept of
the immortal soul. The soul appeared as the essential
and indestructible kernel of a person because it shared
in the knowledge of eternal ideas and their immutable
nature. To say that this soul was immortal was one way
of building up a perpetual present. Human beings did
not really die; their souls simply escaped from their
flesh and blood prisons. Change, in this perspective,
was of little worth. Identity did not reside in their continual and progressive transformation, but in parti-

cipation in what never changed—the world of eternal ideas. There was no promised land to strive for; true identity was given once for all in the immortal soul. They had only to conform to eternal ideas and eternal laws. This world-view, contemplating the divine, drained off energy from the gods; it was not historical. Historiographers did little more than erect monuments to superior beings who defied time in their eternal ideals and norms. Few—perhaps none at all, really— historians of that culture charged themselves to present events in life as examples of human progress and transformation.

Historical understanding of human beings appeared relatively late; it was found first in Israel, certainly the first Mediterranean people for whom the future became the fundamental category of thought. For Israel, no present or past event made any sense if it was not clarified by the light of the Promise. Present events had no real importance unless they were motivated by hope. Israel discovered its identity and its vocation only by looking at its history. Even its accounts of its origins in the call of Abraham or in the creation stories were already impregnated with messianic and eschatological elements. What counted for Israel was the end of its journey. Its community centered more on what was yet to come than on what had already happened.

What was the foundation for this futuristic self-understanding? Unquestionably, it was the notion of God proper to Israel. Yahweh, whose actions were always new, disconcerting, and filled with surprise, was the God of power in freedom. He was not the God of immutable law. The primary expression of his power was creation, where, in his sovereign freedom, he fashioned from the void a multitude of beings he enabled to perpetuate and develop. Man, the masculine and feminine creature, who was the crowning of this creation, was to work and create like the Creator in whose image he was made. But the final and ultimate expression of God's freedom and power was the fulfillment of individual persons and the people as a whole in the resurrection from the dead. The theological synthesis relating creation to resurrection came relatively late in Israel. Most of Israel's literature concentrated on the march of history between these two points. God led his people as a king led his army. There was no participating in this God by contemplation of eternal ideas. One had to join him "on the march" in unreserved confidence and faith. Such commitment expected anything and everything from God—even the most unpredictable things. But it also expected his faithfulness in every trial and difficulty. So creating was this God that historical change could almost be called one of his attributes. By historical change I do not mean anarchy, disorder, or caprice. I refer to those mutations stirred up in the midst of continuity. The God of Israel was both change and continuity. He continued to create and intervene, but his promises remained immutable. They gave rise to a future finality for Israel's existence and became the foundation for history's continuity.

With the advent of Jesus, Judaeo-salvation history, already so different from the Hellenistic world-view, received an even more radical qualification. The early Christians believed that Jesus was the sudden entry of the future into the present. In him was the end of all history, the resurrection from the dead. For this reason Jesus was the Christ and the Lord; in himself he summed up the history of Israel and, from there, the history of the world. This "summing up" in no way implied that each individual was now to dissolve into a collective "Christic" body. On the contrary, what each person was to do was graft his own history to that of Jesus. Precisely in this way did the individual partake in universal salvation history. In other words, the only gate to the Christian community was personal faith in the living Christ. Through faith-participation in the life and death of Jesus one entered both the Kingdom and the Church announcing that Kingdom. In saying this we have already touched upon the baptismal teaching found in St. Paul's epistles that we will treat later on.

At this point in our reflections, it will be helpful to turn to Pannenberg's thesis on the origin of man's historical consciousness.[7] Pannenberg, convinced that the biblical discovery of history was the birth of universal history, maintains that the Judaeo-Christian historical vision first set forth the concept of unity as attainable for all peoples. Profiting from the communication structures of the Roman Empire, this concept moved throughout the Mediterranean world and then to Europe as a whole. Although dwindling during the centuries in which Christianity succumbed to anarchism and immobility, it has reawakened in modern times. Even though more secularized in form since the Enlightenment, it has remained an active force in Western philosophies of history. Its presence is discernible even in Marx's historical dialectic, particularly as articulated by the neo-Marxists.

It is not too pretentious to list process philosophy and the philosophy of solidarity among this tradition's secular fruits. Faith in the God who works within all of man's journeys effectively prepared the Western European mind for a system of thought with such themes as development, planning, and unification. Naturally, the secularization process, cut away the religious premises. The Church, finding itself no longer presiding over mankind's journey and destiny, tended to fall back on eternal values in a somewhat Platonic perspective. Hellenistic immobility began to replace Judaeo-Christian progress in the Church's attitudes, and the rupture between Christianity and a progress-oriented world grew more severe.

The present world situation shows clearly the catastrophic consequences of that rupture. The secular world, adopting an historical understanding for its credo, has entered into an immense task of development and unification. From the Christian perspective, however, the secular world is like a plane gone wild, ejecting its builder and its pilot.[8] Man has set himself up as the guarantee of his own history, and he finds fewer and fewer reasons to believe in himself as history's guarantee. He discovers, for instance, that the equilibrium based on fear and an approximately equal partition of nuclear arms is too fragile for his own peace of mind. He knows, too, that programs of development and unification have not succeeded; in fact, the gulf between nations grows deeper.

What the secularized historical understanding of man needs is the perspective it can never find in its own man-centered anthropology. It needs connection with the God who engenders history and gives it meaning. The Church, for its part, needs to become once again the proclaimer of the bond between the God of history and the history of man. It must put forward the Judaeo-Christian evidence that the transcendent God is immanent in man's relationships and in his time. The Church, by entering into mankind's journeys and crises, witnesses to the immanence of God and gives to man-

kind's progress a point of reference and an inner dynamism beyond itself.[9]

The Church's mission of evangelization, in this
perspective, is translated into actions of progress and
development. The decision for or against Jesus Christ,
consequently, is not simply a matter of abstract Chris-
tological theory and doctrine. It is a recognition that
Jesus Christ has a central place in mankind's history
and means entering into mankind's progress and development.

Baptism, therefore, is much more than a simple ecclesiastical initiation rite or an act of Christian peda-
gogy. It is the sacrament of human historicity, centered
on the God of history, made flesh in Jesus of Nazareth.
Such a definition of the sacrament may seem too minimally ecclesial. Because it does not focus on the now
universally practiced custom of infant baptism, it may
give the impression that it is impractical and utopian—
and it may be. But perhaps the time has come to turn
our baptismal focus from our tender feelings toward a
new-born child to our decision for or against the God of
history and the dynamism of universal progress he demands. The question is valid: How can we speak of integrating personal history into universal history when
the person baptized has no understanding of what is
going on? Even if we theologize about baptism in considering only adult baptism, can we conclude that this
rite of initiation and commitment is the sacrament of
human historicity created by the God of history?

Lest this notion cause shock and misunderstanding, we must now examine the witnesses from the
New Testament and tradition to see the validity of this
perspective on baptism. My thesis that baptism is the
sacrament of human historicity is not really all that

revolutionary. I am not trying to promote baptism as some sort of "super" sacrament. I wish simply to apply the contemporary theological notions of historicity to the meaning of the sacrament.

2
Baptism in Biblical
and Patristic Tradition

To designate Christian baptism's specific character, we must first look at the various purification and
initiation rites practiced at the beginning of our epoch.
Next we shall examine the principal New Testament
texts attesting to the anthropological context in which
the first Christians developed their baptismal theology.
Then, we shall look at the change of perspective that
the early patristic evidence brings to the New Testament understanding of the sacrament. In a final
chapter we shall discuss present-day problems and concerns.

I
PRE-CHRISTIAN PURIFICATION RITES
AND THEIR ANTHROPOLOGICAL FOUNDATIONS[10]

Modern ethnology has given us remarkable evidence for the important role that water played in ancient religions. As a sign of life it symbolized both the
earth's fertility and the fecundity of human and super-
human life. It was also used to produce sacral, cultic,
and ritual purity. Life, in these religions, depended
upon the gods; it came from the celestial world and

there it tended to return. Water, the element signifying biological life and often making it possible, served to symbolize and even produce the cultic state in which man could enter into a relationship with the divine. Thus, water came to be the instrument of cultic, sacral, ritual purity. What is important to remember is the pronounced "verticalism" of these pre-Christian ablutions. They scarcely allude to a journey from past to present to future. They look only to capturing the energies of a superterrestrial world and thereby entering into abundant life. Their anthropology was singularly non-historical.

In the mystery religions, for instance, water purifications were part of a ritual entirely centered on an after-life. Religious man set his eyes on the transcendent, hoping at least to imitate the divine being, if not actually fuse with him. What counted was the divinity's beatifying presence—nothing else. In the Egyptian mystery cult of Osiris, the initiate sought mystical identification with the god. Osiris, a god who died and rose to life again, brought this same hope of passing from death to life. The future, as a contingency to be created, did not even enter the picture. If there was movement, it was only upward to the divinity. The only journey was the mystical voyage to the god.

To the extent that this viewpoint was penetrated by belief in the immortality of the soul, it led directly to dualism. The only true life was the life of the soul, to be achieved by various "techniques" of purification. Purification from what? From carnal existence—earthly and inferior, because changing and linked to perishable matter. The Mandean "baptist" sect typified this point of view.

When we compare these ancient pagan religions

with the Bible, the anthropological difference is immediately obvious. In the mystery religions historical myth dictates everything. People are asked to stop the course of time and flee to eternity (even though they may seek to assure themselves some kind of biological existence in the interim). The quest for immortality dominates this religious view of man; there is no room for a process to build up any temporal or relational history.

In the Old Testament the picture changes.[11] One finds, to be sure, numerous ritual ablutions in the Old Testament—water being used to purify objects and persons. These washings do not, however, look simply to cultic purity facilitating contact with the sacred. What is sought is a permanent, interior relationship between the faithful and their God. The prophets, for instance, insist that true purification is itself a gift of the God who comes to his people continually and who will bring all things to their fullness at the end of time (Jer. 4:4; Ezek. 36:25). God it is who baptizes and bathes his people as they await his coming, walking in pilgrimage toward him. The ablution, then, is eschatological, anticipating a full renewal of human hearts and imposing serious ethical demands. So serious are these demands that a person will be able to accomplish them only by steps, in a constantly renewed movement of conversion and progress.

Special mention must be made, too, of Jewish proselyte baptism.[12] Later Judaism created this rite, called "tebilah," for admitting pagan converts to the community of Israel. In practice about the same time as the early Christian Church, it brought a further anthropological refinement to the origins of Christian baptism: the emphasis on freedom. No one was baptized into Judaism until he knew what commitment he

was making. The ritual, intended to complement circumcision in males and supplant it in females, was
given but once and consisted of a multi-phased cat-
echumenate—instruction and examination leading to
a "profession of faith." But this baptism was not re-
stricted to adult converts; it was administered also to
infants. Children could receive baptism with their con-
vert parents; in fact, they were obliged to, since the patriarchal principle and family solidarity were in full
sway. But rabbinic commentaries underscore a very interesting particularity at this point: infants "Judaized"
in this manner, once they reached the age of their majority, could renounce their relationship with Israel and
return to their ancestors' religion.[13] Jewish tribunals
had no right to force them to remain if they had no personal belief in the community.

What we find here is another instance of anthropological historicity. The proselyte, integrated into the
community, *could* be compared to an entirely new
being, carrying a new name and having nothing to do
with his past. But he is not considered this way. He is a
being in motion between his past, his present, and his
future. Far from being fixed, defined, and catalogued,
he is still susceptible to change. His new situation is
only the point of departure for his journey. He will
meet crossroads and forks in the road, and he may
choose to turn back.

As a conclusion to this section, before turning to
the baptism of John, we must glance at the purification
rites practiced in the Qumran communities.[14] There the
perspective of anthropological historicity, so strong
both in the Old Testament and in the practice of Jewish
proselyte baptism, grows singularly more narrow. In
these sectarian groups, the ablutions, repeated daily,

had only a propitiatory effect. The Essenes, with their highly pronounced sense of sin, sought constantly to re-enter a state of sanctity to be always ready for the Spirit's eschatological intervention (cf IQS 4:21). The great perspective of salvation as history opened by the prophets never succeeded in bringing light to their penitential bathings. For that to occur, John the Baptist had to enter the scene. In him we find the precursor of Christian baptism.

II
BAPTISM IN THE NEW TESTAMENT

The Baptism of John in the Gospel

The Baptist's preaching has all the qualities of a general mobilization. The Kingdom is about to come, a time of judgment, discernment, and choice (Mk. 1:2). The world's Judge is to enter the scene to separate the wheat from the chaff. No arrival date is set, for God is free and he will inaugurate his Kingdom when he pleases. John urges a change of attitude to prepare for this event. The God of freedom must be met with readiness; the change of attitude means standing prepared for his coming at any moment of the night or day and working actively for his arrival: "Prepare ye," he says, "the way of the Lord."

John's "bridge and roadway" images express an eminently historical perspective on God's relationship to man. God's future coming is presented as constitutive of man's being. For the encounter between man and God will not take place on the public squares, but in man's heart, in the very depth of his existence. John's preparatory work is properly called "metanoia," a change of heart. An interior realignment is demanded, the kind of inner choice that remakes a man from top to bottom. The revolution of the Gospels, itself thoroughly historical, is already being proclaimed.

John presents this entire event as the work of God's Spirit, already established in Judaic tradition as the master of the messianic and the eschatological era when history's end-point and finality will flow into the present to give light and clarity. With John, everything that is today is confronted with what it must become in its full and final form. Temporal historicity is condensed into a Spirit-filled present.

The arrival of God's Spirit, however, does not affect only man's temporal historicity. His relational historicity is stirred up as well. Man's relation to man is affected by the essentially universal character of John's preaching. He offers his baptism to all, without distinction of race, religion, or social class.

In this regard, it is significant that the evangelists allude to Isaiah's servant poems in presenting John's baptism of Jesus. The voice from heaven announces: "Behold my servant. . . . I have put my Spirit upon him, and he will bring forth justice to the nations" (Is. 42:1). The Messiah, therefore, will not be a Davidic king or Aaronic priest reserved for Israel's elite, as the Qumran sectarians had hoped. Jesus will be the Messiah for all peoples; by placing himself sinless in the midst of sinful humankind, he will accomplish in his actions the justification that Isaiah's suffering servant had announced in words. In his baptism he submits to John's rite of conversion and thereby enters into relational solidarity with all humankind, itself in need of conversion. In this deed Jesus reveals already the meaning of Christian baptism.

John's baptism therefore fits into the context of universal salvation history. The early Christians, recounting the story of John, could have presented his baptism as an action charged only with the future and with universality. In other words, John's baptism has the characteristics of both temporal and relational historicity and as such prefigures Christian baptism.

The Acts of the Apostles

In the Acts of the Apostles Luke gives us a document reflecting both the origins of the Christian community and its consolidation into a structured Church. In both phases we are confronted with a community conscious of its temporal and relational historicity.

The origins appear in the Jerusalem Pentecost account (Acts 2:37-41). At first we meet a feast celebrated only by Jews and proselytes of the capital city and the diaspora. But it is soon followed by other outpourings of the Spirit—first in Samaria and then in the pagan world represented by the household of Cornelius. Together with the extension of salvation on a relational plane, the Church's pentecostal atmosphere is charged with eschatological tension. The disciples speak of the "last days" and give first priority to the decision for or against Jesus Christ. They announce the "Good News" of his resurrection and baptize in his name all who receive his Word and believe in him. Private property is liquidated (an interesting "relational" corollary to this "temporal" experience), and goods are held in common. The "koinonia" is lived with fervor.

Given this state of affairs, one might suspect that ecstasy, the ravishing of souls because of eternity's imminence, would become the community's dominant thrust. But this was not the case. Ecstasy, in fact, remained the exception; the mainstream was charitable and missionary action. No signs are to be found that work stopped or that Christians set in motion a sort of "eschatological strike." Prayer, not ecstasy, joined with work to mark the Christian community. In St. Luke's account of the Church's origins, the eschatological emphasis did not destroy historicity. Even the end of time, apparently imminent to early Christians, was not the heavenly world's breakthrough into time, but the accelerated conclusion of an historical journey. If these early believers thought of the end as simply "no more time," then perhaps they would have folded their arms and plunged into ecstasy. But since they thought of the end as the summing up of time and the fulfillment of every person and every event still marching in time, they tended to live more intensely than ever. Thus history accelerated, conversions multiplied, and joy over the Lord's return overflowed. The great historical tasks of baptismal evangelization and charity totally occupied their spirits. This mentality was to find expression in the Pauline epistles, where anticipation of the parousia went hand in hand with missionary and charitable action.

In the second phase of his work, Luke presents a progressive distancing from the Church's parousial temper to its spirit of conquest and structuralization. Yet here, too, Luke is faithful in preserving both temporal and relational historicity. He shows how the Church, one and indivisible, enters into universal history under the guidance of the apostles and their successors, the presbyters. The Spirit himself becomes an itinerant missionary. He accompanies those who reach out to evangelize Samaria, Ethiopia, Asia, Greece, and the center of the empire, extending the community both in relationship ᵈ in time. In portraying the Church's growth, Luke joins together the Jewish concept of a sovereignly free historical God and the Hellenistic ideas of organization and good order. Yet none of these structures developed, for controlling and coordinating the missionary and charitable activities has an absolute value. Even the Spirit is "free" to dispense with the order he has himself inspired. Perhaps the most striking example of this is the completely extraordinary baptism of St. Paul. Paul, although destined to become the apostle "par excellence," was not baptized by Peter, John or James, but by an obscure, devout layman named Ananias. Otherwise unknown, he welcomes Paul into the Church and reveals to him that he is to be the "vessel of election" to "bring the name of Christ to the Gentiles" (Acts 9:15; 22:15). Here we encounter two important aspects of historicity throwing light on Christian baptism. First, the God of history remains free, intervening when and where he chooses. Secondly, baptism, although becoming ritually structured, is subject to a pluralism of forms, reflective of God's creative freedom.

The Pauline Epistles

In considering the Pauline panorama of baptismal theology, we must distinguish between two principal groups of texts: the two epistles to the Corinthians, and the epistles to the Galatians and the Romans. Finally, we shall treat the epistle to the Ephesians to complete these two groupings on a precise point.[15]

1. The Epistles to the Corinthians

To understand the predominant ideas in the epistles to the Corinthians, we must remember that St.
Paul is fighting against one of the most renowned of all
"anti-historical" heresies, what Conzelmann has aptly
called "protognosticism."[16] Of eclectic Judaeo-
Hellenistic origins, Corinthian "protognosticism" tended toward pneumatic enthusiasm and extraordinary religious experiences of every kind. In Paul's eyes these
"pneumatics" erred by exaggerated individualistic piety
and sacramental quietism.

Their perspective dominated by what we call "verticalism," Paul urged the Corinthians to take up the
spirit of "koinonia" to stress the place of the collective
body of Christ in their religious experience. "For by
one Spirit," he wrote, "we were all baptized into one
body—Jews or Greeks, slaves or free" (1 Cor. 12:13; cf.
also Gal. 3:26-29). He used here the grammatically
concise Greek expression "into one body," indicating
movement toward a goal worth striving for.

What Paul wants to stress is the purpose of baptism, in his mind a constant movement toward fraternal
communion, together with movement in faith toward
the Lord. Baptism, therefore, is not initiation into ecstasy or quietism, but the beginning of an historical
process on the "relational" and "temporal" planes.
This process, moreover, occurs in both the individual
and the community. The individual never finishes moving forward to build up the community; the community,
in turn, never ceases building up the individual. One
stands in need of the other.

Paul's emphasis on baptism's historicity governs,
for instance, his entire theology of charisms, seen by
him as multiple concretizations of the one baptismal

grace. The charisms express in the daily lives of the baptized the one and unique Spirit, building up the community as a whole. Paul constantly emphasizes that spiritual gifts are never for strictly personal use. Private charisms are not charisms at all; all the gifts must contribute to the building up of the community. Perhaps the most striking example of Paul's thought is the gift of speaking in tongues. An ecstatic and mysterious gift, speaking in tongues can be justified only if it is complemented by the gift of interpretation. Only in this way is this charism comprehensible and useful for the entire community of the baptized (1 Cor. 14:13). For the same reason the charism of prophecy is declared to be the most noble to be sought (1 Cor. 14:1), even as much as the most excellent of gifts, charity. Why? Because the prophet does not upbuild himself. He "speaks to men for their upbuilding and encouragement and consolation" (1 Cor. 14:3). This "speaking to men" on God's behalf activates the community's history and thereby tightens the bonds of all who move forward together toward the Christ, the Lord.

The charisms' social, "relational" character appears in many ways, joining together in dialectical tension gifts that could war against one another. The gift of healing the sick or administering goods is to be valued as much as the gift of prayer (1 Cor. 12:28). The charism of marriage fits into the community as much as the charism of virginity (1 Cor. 7:7). Extraordinary spiritual activities blend together with the "charismatic states of life" enjoyed by the apostles, teachers, and administrators (1 Cor. 12:27-30). The entire community, with all its intrinsic complementarities, manifests the "relational historicity" of God's household. Far from being a refuge of quietism, the Church is a social force for the progress of mankind.

From this understanding of Christian existence we can move to speak of a theology of work. Paul himself raises the issue when he refers to his own apostolic work as the exercise of his charism. When he writes: "But it is God who establishes us with you in Christ, and has commissioned us; he has put his seal on us and given us his Spirit in our hearts as a guarantee" (2 Cor. 1:21-22), he tells us that God himself set him apart to proclaim the Good News. He specifies that it is "in Christ" (*eis Christon*) that God has established him as an apostle, just as God established him as a believer "in Christ" at the moment of his baptism. (cf. 1 Cor. 12:13; Rom. 6:3). If this interpretation of Paul's thought is correct, we have here a true instance of temporal historicity in the continuity between Paul's beginning gift of baptism and the on-going gift of his apostolic work. Paul's charism to be the apostle simply develops along the lines of his specific vocation that was begun for him at the moment of his baptism.

This same line of reasoning can be applied to every task a baptized person assumes today. Paul did not hesitate to label as charisms those tasks that we would call today secular or profane: social security for the sick and the poor, administrative government, and community politics. True charismatic activity is still found in these domains—secularization need not imply de-Christianization. Now that labor is no longer seen as the heinous consequence of original sin, but as one factor in the growth of openness and freedom, work itself can be seen as charismatic, serving to fashion the human society upon which the body of Christ must build. God shapes the world only insofar as the world works to shape itself. The form of the shaping may differ from Paul's theocracy to contemporary socialism, but the same historical transformation goes on, with God continuing to work in it. Work is as much redemptive activity as prayer or acts of worship. Paul's historical understanding of baptism also challenges the Corinthian "protognostics" in their ethical appreciation of the sacrament. In their eyes baptism was a title to security —a sort of high-risk life insurance contract against the future. Their sole desire being the accumulation of possessions for eternal life, these spiritualists were anxious to set up a final and optimal point for their earthly journey. They tended to stop the course of time on a particular beatifying presence or a spiritual possession that would solve all problems. Baptism was just that sort of possession, a sort of initiation into the enjoyment of heavenly goods once for all time. Baptism was early retirement, immediate withdrawal from the active life to contemplate the divine mysteries. To take up the language we have used in this study, the sacrament became a dispensation from historicity.

Paul found it totally unacceptable to turn baptism from the sacrament of action to the sacrament of inertia. Taking up the image of Israel's march through the desert and passage through the Red Sea, he wrote: "Our fathers all passed through the sea; all were baptized into Moses. . . . Nevertheless, with most of them God was not pleased; for they were overthrown in the wilderness" (1 Cor. 10:1-4). What Paul was saying, purely and simply, was that baptism guaranteed nothing at all. If it was not followed by perseverance in the journey, or if the baptized installed themselves at this or that spiritual oasis, salvation became pure illusion and the sacrament a fatal mirage.

Paul wanted to condemn any such magical conception of the sacrament. To pretend that this rite automatically conferred spiritualization—a sort of definitive divinization—ran contrary to Paul's pilgrimage ethic.

"Magical" sacramentalism, fundamentally anti-historical, reduced time to the present instant; the past disappeared by wizardry and the future was predetermined by manipulating the present. If baptism was magic, then the baptized were immobilized by the sacrament. Their play had been made and their destiny petrified by the sacrament's indelible mark.

Against this mentality, Paul developed his image of the race. A long-distance runner, he argued, entered the contest not simply to run, but to gain the prize. From the starter's gun to the finish line, all his muscles and will power stretched forward toward his goal. Totally concentrating on bursting ahead in the race, he disciplined himself at an exacting pace. Paul reminded these Corinthian Christians, so prone to sacramental magicism, that they, like him, had to run the race of life that their baptism implied (1 Cor. 9:24-27). He added, moreover, that a Christian did not run for himself alone; he lived in a "relational" situation. "I pummel my body and subdue it," he writes, "lest after preaching to others I myself should be disqualified" (1 Cor. 9:27). Nothing could be less magical or less a theology of inertia than Paul's own baptismal and apostolic history.

Paul was clear, however, that every ethical imperative had to be rooted in dogmatic soil. His baptismal ethic of action, movement, and responsibility is founded on his theology of the cross. Paul places decisive importance on the fact that Christians are baptized in the name of the crucified Christ. In baptism Christians are joined to him whose journey of the cross was for everyone. The significance of the cross, however, is not in the nails, the thorns, or the torture; what the cross means for the baptized is Jesus' disposition in embracing the ambivalence of the human condition. If Paul can write that "Christ died for our sins," the apostle does not mean by "sin" simply personal acts of revolt against God, neighbor, or oneself. His vision is more global, encompassing all the contradiction, brokenness, and alienation characteristic of mankind on its journey. The cross, in its turn, becomes Paul's symbol for Jesus' accepting and taking responsibly the historical dialectic between good and evil. To be baptized in the name of the crucified Christ is to take on without reservation the risks inherent in mankind's pilgrimage. It means accepting responsibly that everything human can lead either to destruction or construction, to hate or love, to the assassination of life or to its burgeoning forth. Furthermore, it means taking on the insecurity and tension that go with living a pilgrimage. Otherwise, one chooses either fatalistic passivity or the magical optimism of the gnostics.

In this theology of the cross, we find ourselves again at the heart of Christianity's historicity. Because human existence justifies neither optimism nor pessimism, there is nothing more human than the cross. Life is bi-polar, stretched in all its atoms between life and death and in all its conscious sectors between good and evil. One can even say that to exist is already to be crucified. What Jesus brings is this: a positive, unreserved, and unconditional acceptance of the human condition that allows for realistic action in order to gain salvation. Suffering certainly helps attain the goal, but so do protests, criticism, and progressive, constructive work. No wonder Paul defends the folly of the cross so passionately against the defleshed wisdom of his adversaries. It is no surprise that he links baptism so closely to living out the crucifixion.

From the theology of the cross we can move directly to the second group of Pauline texts to consider: the epistles to the Romans and the Galatians.

2. The Epistles to the Romans and the Galatians

Paul's baptismal theology in these writings is summed up in these verses: "Do you not know that all of us who have been baptized into Christ Jesus were baptized into his death? We were buried therefore with him by baptism into death, so that as Christ was raised from the dead by the glory of the Father, we too might walk in newness of life" (Romans 6:3-4).

What the apostle here affirms is a break with the past and an opening to the future. The simultaneous character of the two phenomena is important. Nothing permits us to conclude to a sort of "dead time" between the Christian's dying to sin and his rising to walk in new life. Baptism is both end and beginning, the definitive and determining act for the person baptized.

Does Paul give the sacrament an exaggerated, idealistic, utopian significance? No baptized person, after all, remains sinless; he always runs the risk of stopping on his journey in "newness of life." What, moreover, does this concept of the sacrament imply about the life that precedes baptism? Does it not neglect the richness of that period, already filled with many human and religious values? What, too, of those multitudes never baptized, whose resemblance to the Christ often exceeds that of Christians?

To avoid doing Paul an injustice, we must leave aside for the moment this last critical question of the salvation of unbelievers. Paul's perspective does not really speak to that issue. His concern is ethical. He wants to remind Christians already deeply committed to their existence as believers to return to the origins of their Christian way of life. He does not want his readers to believe that ethical emphasis belongs to peccadillos or acts of virtue performed before or after baptism. The Pauline ethic does not consist in an accounting of good or bad thoughts; it is not a comparison of moral with immoral episodes. Paul's is an ethic of action, not of acts. It is an ethic of historicity, journey, and relationship. Its components are movement, community, and free obedience, stemming from a fundamental option on the part of both the community and the individual.

The key to understanding this ethic is the formula "into Christ Jesus," indicating more finality than locality. Here, Paul points very precisely to the person (Christ Jesus) toward whom the baptized believer must direct his faith. The apostle refers to the on-going action of commitment accomplished because of a fundamental option made for Christ. The person baptized "into Christ Jesus" delivers himself so that Christ's history becomes his own. In baptism the Christian takes to himself Christ's own journey and fashions his life from this starting point.

This attitude of faith and confidence is to be distinguished from faith in "God." Paul is proclaiming faith in Jesus, Christ and Lord, born of a woman and crucified. This kind of faith consists of communion with Jesus, the Son of God who embraced the ambivalence of the human condition in its entirety. Believing means entering into solidarity with his free obedience to his Father's will; it means sharing his destiny and espousing his personal history, including his death and resurrection.

There is, consequently, an existential analogy between the destiny of Jesus and that of the baptized. What happened to Jesus will happen to them. The finality of Jesus' history will also be theirs. In their attitudes and experiences of sin, death, grace and life they look to Jesus. In living out their own history, their free obedience to the Father is not so much a series of acts as a total life attitude, perpetuating itself along a continuous existential process.

The over-all Pauline emphasis in Romans is on "life." Even the immediate rupture with the powers of alienation and evil, which in Romans Paul calls "death," is only the first step on a journey. Death's meaning comes from what follows—a pilgrimage marked essentially by life and resurrection. The baptized are reminded that they take this road in companionship with the risen Christ. Paul's pilgrimage image has overtones of an entire program of historicity. "Walking in newness of life" expresses graphically the necessity of going beyond what has been to what will be tomorrow. The Pauline "new man" (Col. 3:9ff.), the bearer of new things and harbinger of the future, is a person of incessant progress in all domains—spiritual, religious, social, and scientific. Achieving their own historicity by reference to Christ's, Christians look to their baptism as the starting point for their ethic of movement, community, and free obedience.

Paul proclaims a similar understanding of baptism's historical, ethical implications in another image used in both Romans and Galatians. He tells the Romans: "Put on the Lord Jesus Christ" (Rom. 13:14), and to the Galatians he writes: "For as many of you as were baptized into Christ have put on Christ" (Gal. 3:27).[17] Is Paul simply taking over an image from the mystery cults in the Hellenistic world, where the custom of clothing the initiates symbolized their mystical identification with the divinity? Or is he borrowing from the Old Testament where one finds expressions like "put on righteousness" and "covered with the robe of righteousness" (Is. 59:17; 61:10)? The exact source of the imagery is difficult to ascertain. But in none of these instances do we meet the Pauline idea of being clothed with another *person.* Probably we are once again in the presence of one of the condensed formulas the apostle loved to create to express the richness of the relationship between believers and Christ. The contexts of Romans and Galatians lean to this meaning. To "put on" Christ is to assimilate him and take on his qualities, to live in his image and likeness.

There is a significant difference in the way the image is used in the two epistles. In Galatians, the apostle speaks in the indicative mood, accentuating the conformity between the life of Christ and the lives of the baptized. "In Christ Jesus," he writes, "all are sons of God through faith. . . . There is neither Jew nor Greek, there is neither slave nor free, there is neither male nor female; for you are all one in Christ Jesus" (Gal. 3:26-28). All the baptized, because of their relationship "in Christ," without distinction of origin, class, or sex, are children of God. When, in the epistle to the Romans, he announces the same message in the imperative mood, Paul reminds Christians that this relationship, although received once for all time, is not a terminated, fulfilled, or totally accomplished reality. In Romans Paul issues a call to action. He presses the baptized to behave as children of God, as brothers and sisters to one another.

His ethical imperative flows from his dogmatic indicative. Christians are to make real in their actions what they are by the gift of God, translating in their personal history what they were made to be at the moment of their baptism. Justified, they are to behave justly. This manner of placing the baptized at a point between a gift and a command fits in perfectly with the condition of historicity in which every human person must walk. The baptized will be able to retain what they have received only if they make the gift of Christ's life and righteousness their life and their hope. God's gifts are historical; they tend to future fulfillment.

All we have said so far in interpreting Romans and Galatians poses a philosophical problem that theology cannot pass by—the problem of contemporaneity. How can the baptized be contemporaries with Christ? If they are not, then the communion of destiny and relationship shared with Christ is inconceivable.

A first element of solution comes from anthropological experience, telling us that relationship transcends time. Two persons in love, for example, give of themselves unreservedly and remain united despite any spatial or temporal distances separating them. A mere sign is enough—a letter, a picture—and the sense of absence is overcome.[18] Evidently this kind of love relationship cannot be postulated between Jesus and the faithful who have never seen him. Paul does not suggest this. Neither for himself nor for his readers does he make his first appeal to a believer's love for Jesus. What he demands as the fundamental attitude is *faith*. He knows that faith can transcend distances because its power comes from the revelation God makes of himself in making clearer the meaning of life. From the moment the believer begins to discover the meaning of his existence, he opens himself up to the God who reveals that meaning. Christians believe in God and trust in him, knowing that without this gift of belief they would never be able to realize their own personal history.

Jesus, revelation incarnate, places life's meaning at mankind's doorstep. In choosing to believe in him, Christians turn toward him with their entire being as they would toward the meaning of life. Temporal distance does not have fundamental significance in such a relationship. From the moment that believers find their personal histories mobilized by Jesus' own history, even centuries of separation no longer constitute a barrier. Why? Because they find in his history the significance of their own existence. In a true and real sense, faith enables "relational historicity" to confer an absolutely new quality to "temporal" historicity. The time factor becomes no longer a separation component, but a bond of union. Time actually becomes servant to the more fundamental faith-relationship, giving Christians a dimension for growth in their pilgrimage with the Lord. Because of faith, Jesus and Christians are contemporaries.

This analysis of how Christians can be contemporary with Jesus in their journey in life may appear too mystical to be real. If, however, we do not emphasize the transcendental character of Christianity's relational and temporal historicity, baptism will hardly differ from initiation into any other society or group dedicated to human progress. The trans-temporal character that faith brings to baptism makes the Christian's life an adventure in community and freedom with Jesus. Faith gives Christians meaning and purpose that go beyond time. By focusing life's significance on Jesus' faith enables Christians to have the security that comes from having a goal clearly in mind.

3. The Epistle to the Ephesians

To discover the key to the baptismal theology proposed in this great epistle, so different in language and in style from the Pauline epistles we have already considered, we must keep two notions in mind: Church and cosmos. Both are collective terms in the author's eyes. Engaged in controversy with gnostics tending toward a philosophy of fullness and completion, the epistle stresses the collective dimensions of Christian existence.

In this regard, nothing is more characteristic than the author's notion of the "new creation." For Paul, this notion had a clearly personal significance (cf. 2 Cor. 5:17; Gal. 6:15), linked closely with his image of "putting on the Lord Jesus Christ." In Ephesians, however, the meaning is clearly collective (Eph. 1:10; 2:10). The author is less concerned with ethical implications than with cosmic meaning. Jesus, for instance, is presented not so much as the object of a personal response of faith, but as the fashioner of the cosmos and the head of the universal Church (cf. Eph. 1:22). The personal question the author raises is: How does the individual relate to the collectivity? The verses of the hymn cited in chapter four are especially significant: "Our Lord, one faith, one baptism, one God and Father of us all, who is above all and through all in all" (Eph. 4:5-6).

Baptism, therefore, is presented as the way to total unity with all peoples and all creation. The obvious danger in this perspective is precisely that the individual believer is no longer the primary consideration. With neither personal faith nor personal ethical response stressed, what matters first of all is the collective relationship between Jesus as master of the world and his

Church. Ephesians looks to the definitive establishment of all things in heaven where (and this is significant in our context) all will be "seated." (We are no longer in Paul's imagery of "walking in newness of life.") Time, in this epistle's vision of things, is less significant than in Romans and Galatians. Past and future are compressed into the present moment. One can hardly speak anymore of "temporal historicity," so absent is the emphasis on passing from one's past to a future to be created. Ephesians emphasizes anticipating what must come, not journeying to create a possible future.

Despite this cosmic and universal emphasis, the personal and provisionary are not entirely discarded. In fact, the author addresses himself to very concrete categories of persons to remind them of baptism's ethical demands. But even in speaking to married persons, children, slaves, and masters, what is most personal is integrated into the author's collective vision. Husbands, for instance, are urged to love their wives, but their love is compared immediately to the love of Christ for the Church. "Husbands," writes the author, "love your wives, as Christ loved the Church and gave himself up for her, that he might sanctify her, having cleansed her by the washing of water with the Word, that he might present the Church to himself in splendor, without spot or wrinkle or any such thing, that she might be holy and without blemish" (Eph. 5:25-27). The author's principal concern is the relationship between Christ and the Church.

Ephesians, then, does not by-pass Paul's historical, ethical demands. The author tells believers that they can solidly attach themselves to Christ, the head of the cosmos and the Church, without losing their own identity. Aware that their fullness is with Christ, they need not cloister in on themselves. Rather, they open their lives to all creation, beginning with those closest to them, spouses, children, masters, slaves.

4. The Later New Testament Writings

In other later New Testament writings, baptism's properly historical perspective also undergoes something of an eclipse. The epistle to the Hebrews, 1 Peter, and the Johannine Gospel, three later documents with many elements of baptismal theology, pull away fairly strongly from an explicitly temporal point of view. Their horizons are set less upon baptism as beginning a pilgrimage and lean more to viewing the sacrament as illumination, purification, and regeneration—notions cherished in the mystery religions and in gnostic cenacles (cf. 1 Pet. 1:3; 2:3: Ti. 3:4-7; Jn. 3:5).

Side by side with their "spiritualistic" or "vertical" vocabulary arises a series of cultic images in reference to baptism: temple, sacrifice, and priesthood. The question arises: Does the development of these aspects of baptism—visionary, intellectual, and cultic—run contrary to Judaeo-Christianity's fundamentally historical orientation? If not, do these writings at least suggest a revision or nuancing of what we have said so far about the historicity of Christian existence? Should not the significance of baptism be interpreted more mystically? Should we not see the sacrament as more rooted in eternity?

In fact, none of these writings runs contrary to a radically historical understanding of existence, nor is their theology more mystical than that of the apostle Paul. Like Paul, these authors were battling against the

anti-historical tendencies of gnosticism and proto-gnos-
ticism. But their emphasis is different from Paul's.
They are more concerned with deepening the present
experience than with concentrating on a future to be
created. John's writings, for instance, emphasize actual
faith decisions and the actual coming of the Holy
Spirit. In developing their cherished symbols of temple
and cult there is no doubt that their emphasis is on the
here-and-now, "vertical" relationship between the believer and Christ. Unlike the anti-historicists they were
opposing, however, these later New Testament writers
do not opt for anti-historical belief. Everything they say
in their mystical and cultic terminology demands practice and follow-through as much as the pilgrim, itinerant baptismal perspective advanced by Paul and Luke.
Even the mystical temple in 1 Peter is not a static heap
of stone, but a living body of living stones never ceasing
to grow.

What really predominates in these writings (and
saves them from running contrary to Paul's and Luke's
earlier ideas) is an emphasis on "relational" historicity
centered on the living Christ. Because of the situation
in which they were written, they emphasized less the
believer's "becoming" responsibilities and focused attention on Christ as the source and origin of personal
belief. They sought to preserve the sacrament from tendencies to reduce the entire Christian message to another form of intellectualized humanism. In saying, for
instance, that no one can see the Kingdom of God
unless he is fashioned by God and born again from "on
high" (Jn. 3:3-8), John's Gospel stood against the gnostics of that day and their esoteric, magical techniques of
spirituality. These authors, in affirming that without
the divine Spirit's illumination the human spirit re-

mains in darkness, maintain that God's prevenient
grace and power indispensably precede every human
endeavor. Truly salvific action, they insist, has its primary source in God. Christians, in their steps to the future, depend radically upon their historical rendezvous
with God. This perspective links closely with Paul's and
Luke's emphasis on the pilgrimage of the baptized.
Practically speaking, this means that Christians continue to live out their baptism in movement, community, and freedom so that their capacities for the future
can be unleashed.

Baptismal Theology in the Second Century[19]

To complete our investigation into the origins of
baptismal theology, we must now look briefly into the
picture presented in the patristic documents up to the
turn of the second century. This inquiry will lead us
into our consideration of contemporary problems and
issues, since the structures of baptism that need reform
today were crystallized in those early times. The documents we shall consider—the Didache, the epistle of
Pseudo-Barnabas, the epistles of Ignatius of Antioch,
and some of the writings of Justin, Irenaeus, and Tertullian—trace the principal lines of theological evolu-
tion in a veritable mosaic of diverse cultures, personali-
ties, situations, and literary forms.

In the Didache, for instance, we find the manifestation of later Judaism's stress on law and ritual. This
document, really a Christianized version of the Jewish
ritual for proselyte baptism, concentrates on ceremoni-
al order, conditions for admission to baptism, and ritual distinctions between, for instance, infusion and im-
mersion. What is so striking about its witness is the

almost total absence of any theological perspective, especially the lack of Pauline thought!

The epistle of Pseudo-Barnabas does give a certain theological perspective, but one heavily cloaked in Alexandrian symbolism. Life's goal is the spiritual understanding of things, and baptism is merely one component of a perfect "gnosis." Rebirth and re-creation are the principal baptismal themes, and the Scriptures are to be searched for these images. Once found, they are applied allegorically to the sacrament. For our purposes, we must note that this kind of allegory attaches absolutely no importance to historicity. The rebirth and re-creation events of the Old Testament are not integral to the history of salvation; they simply point to what has been fully accomplished and revealed in Christ. The past does not live on in the present, and the future is irrelevant, since the blessed possession of the divine is achieved in baptism and faith. Pseudo-Barnabas, in its turn, leads us away from the New Testament's historical understanding of the sacrament.

With Ignatius of Antioch we find equal emphasis on God's immediate relationship to man. What colors Ignatius' thought is his own imminent martyrdom. His own desire for eternity so impregnates his writings that his death, not baptism, seems to be his fundamental freeing action. He refers to himself as "dying into Christ" (ad Rom. 6:1), just as Paul, in his epistle to the Romans, had referred to being "baptized into Christ" (Rom. 6:3). In the same manner, Ignatius delights in transferring baptismal terminology and symbolism to his physical death. He refers to his death as his "coming to birth," the act by which he receives "pure light" and becomes an "imitator of the passion" of his God (ad Rom. 6:1-3).

Ignatius also brings a marked dualism to his

"death-baptism" perspective. Death, because it gives access to the Father, is the saint's victory of eros, desire, and the love of the material world. To be fair to Ignatius we must note that it is martyrdom—death fully accepted as a witness to Christ—that receives all these baptismal qualities. But the totality of his mystical, symbolic affirmations do not reflect the kind of respect for human history and progress we have stressed in presenting the New Testament theology of baptism. The sole Ignatian passage commenting on Jesus' baptism in the Jordan, for instance, says that if Jesus indeed was baptized, it was to "purify the waters by his passion" (Eph. 18:2). There is nothing here to indicate Jesus' entry into the history of God's action among men. Water, in Ignatius' mind, a material element undoubtedly inhabited by demonic powers, has to be purified and even exorcised before it can become a sacramental sign. Like all creation, sacraments exist only to reflect God's plan to deliver men from the world of matter and lead them to eternity.

The same kind of dualistic thinking appears in his letter to Polycarp where baptism is compared to a shield (Polycarp 6:2). Baptism becomes a defensive weapon, a means of protection against the demons. Numerous other passages speak of the battle to be fought against evil spirits (Eph. 17:1; Magn. 1:2; Trall. 4:2; Rom. 7:1; Philad. 6:2). Finally, the Antiochian martyr brings his passion for order into his baptismal thought. The sacrament, he insists, is in the hands of the bishops and the other ministers. Its administration must be controlled; "free" baptism is forbidden (Smyr. 8:2; Polycarp 6:1-2).

Ignatius' baptismal legacy has obvious value in the history of spirituality and in developing a Christian theology of death. Because of his enormous stature in the history of church structure, however, his baptismal work has proved to be a seminal contributor to a highly dis-incarnate baptismal theology. His writings in this area do not admit of an historical perspective. Despite numerous scriptural citations, he does not espouse the fundamentally historical New Testament theology of the sacrament.

Still other theological concepts came to be added to the significance of baptism in the second century. Clement of Rome, the Pastor of Hermas, and the so-called Second Epistle of Clement brought forth a new note by their emphasis on the pentitential aspect of the sacrament. The second century witnessed the development of an extremely animated controversy over the readmission of apostates and public sinners to the ecclesial community. The two documents bearing Clement's name seem to favor the rigorist response already formulated in the canonical epistle to the Hebrews: "For it is impossible to restore again to repentance those who have once been enlightened, who have tasted the heavenly gift, and have become partakers of the Holy Spirit" (Heb. 6:4). The "Clementine" documents appear to hold to this rule. Baptism, they contest, is the one and unique repentance; it is like Noah's ark, welcoming its passengers only once (1 Clem. 7:6; 9:4). Moreover, outside the ark one could do nothing but perish. Reflecting the ideas of Ignatius of Antioch, these letters indicate that baptism must be "guarded." Why? Because it conveys a perfect gnosis and an immaculate character. Here we encounter a classic conservative stance. Beware of the risks of the journey, we are told. The treasure received in baptismal illumination must be preserved from every attack of evil. And its loss would be irreparable.

Evidently such purism and perfectionism would

provoke a reaction in an era when persecution was beginning to bring to light the fallibility of large numbers of the baptized. The Pastor of Hermas, in its penitential tolerance, was the most outstanding expression of this reaction. This work, although maintaining that baptism must be seen as the fundamental repentance, insists that it is not the only repentance. The baptized who fall into sin have not lost every chance of being saved. They can be admitted officially to a second conversion. In other words, they can renew the dispositions they had at the time of their baptism.

The author of Hermas, in addition to his somewhat revolutionary stand on renewed repentance, reveals another engaging trait. He does not hesitate to take us into his confidence, presenting himself sometimes as a great sinner and sometimes as already a saint—a veritable "simul justus et peccator" even before the term arose! He tells us how he continues to fall and to rise up again. His entire life appears to be a continual repentance. Together with other "sinner-saints," he fluctuates between great severity and pronounced self-indulgence (cf. Prec. IV, 3:1-7; Visions III, 7:3-4; Simil. VIII, 6:3; IX, 16:1-4).

Hermas' almost autobiographical details possess a theological significance that is in no way negligible. For, unlike so many of his second-century contemporaries, he moves once again in the direction of an historical understanding of Christian, baptismal existence.

With Justin Martyr this historical perspective again falls into the background. Baptism is presented as an illumination—the acquisition of "gnosis," the true knowledge of God. The realm of ignorance is abandoned in baptism for the realm of true doctrine (Dial. 13-14; 1 Apol. 61). Justin's Platonic outlook is certainly unfavorable terrain for an historical perspective on the Christian life. He presents Christians as illuminated and regenerated at the very instant of their baptism. "This washing," he writes, "is called an illumination." He then adds: "Those who are convinced and believe what we say is the truth . . . we lead to a place where there is water, and they are regenerated" (1 Apol. 61). Although this Christian philosopher does note that candidates for baptism must learn how to pray and to ask God's pardon for their sins, he does not take into account the dialectic of often crucifying events that precede and follow the instant the sacrament is received. He does speak, it is true, of a period of catechesis preceding baptism, but he does not speak of that long journey in "newness of life" that Pauline anthropology identified with post-baptismal life. Believers are not presented as pilgrims on the road to perfection. On the contrary, they appear as already transformed in the present without much need to grow in the future. With Justin, therefore, Christian historicity does not really enter the scene.

Irenaeus of Lyons (c. 202 A.D.) brings another development to baptismal theology. In combat with the gnostics of his day, he adopts a "return to the incarnation" theme, seeking to integrate carnal reality with the mystery of Christ. Since redemption means for him the recapitulation and divinization of all creation, the incarnation is itself redemptive. His over-all theological approach, vital and optimistic, appears significantly in his baptismal theology: "For as a lump of dough cannot be fashioned of dry wheat without liquid matter—nor can a loaf possess unity—neither can we, being many, be made one in Christ Jesus without the water from heaven. . . . For our bodies have received unity among themselves because of the washing that leads to incorruption, and our souls, because of the Spirit. Wherefore both are necessary, since both contribute toward the life of God" (Adv. Haer. III, 17, 2).

This text reflects admirably Irenaeus' synthesis, where matter interpenetrates with the Spirit of God. (Teilhard de Chardin must have shouted for joy in reading this text!) Irenaeus borrows from the world of biology its images of vitality, health, unity, and fecundity. In this optimistic aura, both water and the Spirit of God are indispensable for people to advance in their faith existence. No Platonic dualism here—the human rite and God's power embrace to bring about unity and the life of God in people. Irenaeus does not simply state that material reality is not evil and can therefore be an instrument of God's Spirit. No, the material element of baptism is itself of divine origin; it is "the water from heaven" and "leads to incorruption," forming all the baptized into one body. God's material creation joins with his Spirit to unleash an historical process culminating in the resurrection of the flesh.

The sainted bishop of Lyons preserves in an original manner the historicity of Christian existence. He takes earthly realities seriously. Far from being obstacles to salvation, they are its component parts, essential to any process of integration. From his writings on baptism we can move easily to theologies of the body, sexuality, pleasure, and work. In baptism God's Spirit and his material creation join together to begin the historical process that will culminate in the resurrection of the flesh.

We must point out one area of caution. Irenaeus appears optimistic to the point of unreality. Very little in his baptismal thought points to the setbacks, ruptures, and failures that the baptized inevitably meet in their pilgrimage. Contemporary theology no longer sees baptism as simply a moment in an harmonious process called recapitulating all things in Christ. Today, baptism is also seen as a sign of contradiction and a dramatic event. Just what this implies concretely will be treated in our third chapter. Here we want to note only the apparent absence of the opposition between the finite and the infinite in Irenaeus' thought. This opposition, constitutive of every being and of every movement of being, is not the same as the Platonic distinction between matter and spirit. Nor is it to be identified with little nuanced ethical systems pairing off good against evil. We have already referred to the "dialectic" in the historical process. Existentially positive and contributing to growth in movement, community, and freedom, it can also give rise to disintegration, destructive antagonisms, and loss of freedom. Irenaeus overlooks this tension. He leaves us, it is true, with an historical perspective thoroughly valuable in relating baptism to the incarnation and the redemptive process. But his optimism puts us on guard lest we fall into naiveté in trying to formulate an adequate baptismal theology. Where, for Irenaeus, the sacrament was almost entirely a moment of triumph and a festival of unity, contemporary theology must emphasize its role as another starting point in a corporate and individual journey that includes suffering, death, and resurrection.

Our last second-century witness also brings an historical emphasis to the sacrament of baptism, but with his own originality and limitations. Tertullian (c. 202) brings to his theology both the jurist's realism and the conservative ethicist's severity. As a jurist (an expert in individual rights in Roman law) he considers baptism as a Roman "sacramentum"—a contractual commitment. Consequently his emphasis centers on the sacrament as an institutionally ecclesial action. He does not hesitate to compare baptism to the oath Roman soldiers took upon entering the empire's service or to the oral deposition made by litigants before a tribunal. Some of Tertullian's influence will find its way into the sixteenth century in Zwingli's writings, and be renewed in the twentieth century by Karl Barth in his objections to infant baptism.[20]

In his idea of contract, Tertullian does not have in mind modern ideas of personal freedom and individual responsibility. In comparing Christians to voluntarily enlisted soldiers, he emphasizes the ideas of discipline and fidelity belonging to his time. Since there was no room for individual questioning or personal judgments once soldiers had enlisted, Tertullian demands that baptismal commitments be made only by those fully aware of what they are about. In speaking of infant baptism, his concern for the contract is clear: "It is true our Lord says, 'Do not hinder their coming to me.' So let them come, but only when they are growing up, learning, and being taught what they are coming to; let them be made Christians when they are able to know Christ" (De Baptismo, 18:5). Obviously he insists that there must be knowledge of what the baptismal commitment is before children can be admitted to the sacrament.

Tertullian has another concern. The renouncing of sin, so much a part of his baptismal theology, is of such importance that he prefers baptism not be administered at all if it is to be contradicted by later activity. "All who understand baptism's weighty nature," he continues, "will have more fear of obtaining it than of postponing it" (De Baptismo, 18:6).

Here the jurist joins with the ethicist. Salvation is so serious and dramatic a reality that its plea must be made by the candidate himself. Furthermore, baptism brings with it so many ethical demands that authorities are not to offer the sacrament to the weak, the incapable, or the ill-prepared. It is to be reserved for a well-trained elite. One wonders, in this vision of things, just where God's grace is to be found. Where is his sovereign freedom saving precisely the weak, the incapable, and those who from a certain point of view never will be "well prepared"? In posing this question, I am not seeking to diminish the value of personal commitment as a strong and important component in any realistic, historical understanding of baptism. What Tertullian fails to stress adequately, however, is the absolute gratuity of God's grace. Taken by itself, Tertullian's witness to baptism leads to an elitist and voluntaristic rigorism more stoical than authentically Christian. Christianity, realizing what man is and what his capabilities and limits are, welcomes everyone. The drama of salvation is not reserved for an elitist minority. Baptism's demands, it is true, may in no way be possible for everyone, but in a special way baptism can claim for itself the Gospel's words: "What is impossible to man is possible for God." We can almost call baptism the sacrament of the Christian challenge, the sign that the baptized are called in a fundamental way to climb to the summit of their historical journey. They are to grow in awareness of who they are; although not an elitist group, they receive an elitist call. They are marked as pioneers—the avant-garde, ready for action.

Despite its elitist tendencies, Tertullian's understanding of the sacrament retains a fundamentally historical bias. His emphasis on the baptismal "contract" implies a journey with struggles and a final prize. Had he been able to purge his thought of its rigorist and elitist tendencies, he would have been an even more salutary antidote against the second-century attempts to "de-historicize" baptism's meaning and significance.

What comes clearly to the fore in the total picture of these second-century witnesses to baptism is their evident distancing from biblical (especially Pauline) thought. Diminished (or at least put aside in importance) is the dialectical tension between baptism as gift and as call to action implied in Paul's imagery of "putting on the Lord Jesus Christ." What we have pointed out as an eminently historical understanding of Christian existence modifies and even changes for the worse in ritualism (the Didache), Platonic dualism (Pseudo-Barnabas, Ignatius of Antioch), mystical intellectualism (Justin Martyr), and juridicism penetrated by the spirit of Roman law (Tertullian).

Each of these influential thinkers represents an attempt to implant the Christian message in a different cultural situation, but the resulting theological pluralism has not always been taken into account. Traditional Scholastic theology, for instance, tended to place them all in a straight, evolutionary line of thought, forgetting that each was conditioned by his own historical limitations. Contemporary theology seeks more to criticize each one in his own strengths and weaknesses from themes fundamental in biblical revelation. Such has been our intention in reviewing them from the perspective of baptismal historicity.

In view of this central theme of historicity, we must now turn our attention to a particular element found in the different baptismal theologies we have investigated—the recurrent theme of "sin." The second-

century Church Fathers, as much as the biblical authors, take for granted that baptism presupposes the
subject's conversion and God's forgiveness of sin. Even
the most "optimistic" witnesses, such as Irenaeus, do
not depart from this conviction. In none of them, however, do we meet the idea of "original sin." Our sources
take into account only those faults committed personally by candidates for baptism together with what they
call the "sin of the world," the power of evil in the
world from which baptism rescues man. It could be
argued that these early Fathers did not treat "original
sin" in their baptismal writings because they were entirely preoccupied with adult baptism. But such was not
the case. Toward the end of the second century, infant
baptism was already in evidence as an on-going practice. Tertullian, as we noted, expressed reservations
about this practice. What we can say is that the association of original sin with infant baptism does not
possess the same antiquity as the association of personal sin with adult baptism.

In truth, the origin   in-infant baptism association
came only later in the sacrament's history, first evi-
denced at the Synod of Carthage (c. 253 A.D.). The
synod leaders rejected the proposal of putting off baptism until the eighth day after birth, as had been the
case with circumcision, decreeing that infants were to
be baptized the second or third day after birth. To wait
any longer, they insisted, would be dangerous because
of original sin. St. Cyprian reported the synod's mind:
"We all judge that the mercy and grace of God must be
denied to no man born," adding that although infants
had not sinned personally, nevertheless they had "con-
tracted the contagion of the first death" (Ep. 64:2-6).

A century and a half later St. Augustine will build

from this synodal decision a coherent theology of original sin that will be the masterpiece in his polemic
against the Pelagians. He is the first to speak habitually
of "original sin" and the first to attribute blamewor-
thiness to it, specifying its character as a fault shared
by father and children alike because transmitted by insemination (*Contra Julianum, op. imp.* I, 98). All new-
born children, therefore, inherit this state of sin; they
are born blameworthy. Not only do all new-born children inherit this state of sin, but their congenital blame-
worthiness is already present in the act of sexual union
which transmitted the fault. In Augustine's eyes the act
of sexual union is never free from perverse libido (*De
nuptiis et concupiscentia,* I, 24, 27; *Contra Julianum,*
6:22). Because of this sin, committed first by the father
of the human race and inherited by all his descendants,
the nature of every new-born child is "wounded, sick,
and destined to torment and loss" (*De nat. et grat.,* 62).
The essence of this sin resides in concupiscence, that
constant rebellion of people's lower energies against
their reason, together with their aversion from God (*De
pecc. meritis,* 2:4; *Contra Julianum,* 2, 3, 5). All children thus belong to the "massa damnata"; should they
die without baptism they are lost (cf. *De orig. animae*
3, 9, 12; *Ep.* 196, 28). The only hope Augustine leaves
for them he calls "damnatio mitissima," the most mild
form of loss (*De pecc. meritis,* 1, 21). To strengthen
and validate this theory of original sin, Augustine refers
to the universally widespread practice of infant baptism. If the Church does not believe in original sin, he
argues, why does it baptize new-born children?

What can we say about this theory? First we must
look to Augustine's basic intentions, and especially his
desire to explain the problem of evil. His was the world

of the decline of the Roman empire and the waves of barbarian invasions. The universality of moral evil had to be accounted for lest weary men impute evil to God himself. Secondly, Augustine wanted to refute the Pelagians, whose teachings tended to make salvation dependent upon human strength alone; God's grace, they said, simply aided what man himself accomplished. Pelagius, an ascetical monk, proposed a naive optimism so rigorous and terribly demanding that it risked leaving masses of people, incapable of the super-human efforts he required, lost in hopeless despair. What Augustine sought to preserve in his doctrine of original sin was the universality of God's goodness—he could not ascribe evil's origins to God—and the absolute gratuity of God's salvation. Redemption, he insisted, was not dependent upon human efforts. Despite his basic intentions, however, there were important weaknesses in his thesis.

Even the magisterium of the Church has shown itself more and more cautious in taking over Augustine's thought. The Council of Trent, for instance, disapproved the Augustinian pessimism expressed in some of the theses of Luther and Calvin. Together with the humanists, the council supported the doctrine of free will and omitted the term "concupiscence" in its definition of original sin (Dz 788ff.). The anathemas subsequently pronounced against Baius (Dz 1047-1051) and Jansenism (Dz 1526), followed by the severe criticism of Rosmini's neo-Manicheism (Dz 1923ff), concretized this on-going caution.

Even tradition preceding Augustine made it impossible to establish the kind of indissoluble union between baptism and original sin that he proposed. St. Paul himself stated clearly that children born where at least one parent was Christian were "holy" (1 Cor. 7:14). Tertullian further designated this manner of sanctification as "seminis praerogativa," a prerogative by reason of the seed. Tertullian, in fact, moved in a direction diametrically opposed to Augustine. For the second-century jurist, insemination transmitted holiness, not sin! This idea permitted him to speak of the infancy as the age of innocence, and he asked: "Why should innocent infancy hasten to the forgiveness of sins?" (De bapt. 18, 27).

The little-known Apology of Aristeas (c. 117-138) runs in a similar vein. This document praised the attitudes of persecuted Christians in these terms: "When a child is born to them, they give thanks to God; if that child should die, they give thanks to God beyond all measure that he departed sinless" (13:11).

Among Augustine's own contemporaries, John Chrysostom seemed unaware of original sin in his sermons to neophytes. In scarcely associating the idea of sin to infant baptism, he remained a faithful witness to the majority of opinions in the ancient Oriental tradition.

Contemporary theology is even more critical of Augustine's teaching. This is not the place to enter into an extended discussion of original sin, but a comment on the relationship between Augustine's theory of original sin and this study's theory of historicity is called for. I believe that Augustine's theory is profoundly non-historical in its approach and incompatible with biblical and contemporary anthropology. Four principal points can be advanced in support of this opinion.

1. The historicity of Christian existence consists fundamentally in man's openness and movement toward the future. To the extent that the future takes

shape and becomes accessible, the past clarifies and takes on deeper significance. The Augustinian thesis, rather than focusing on the future, gives undue priority to the past by making Adam's sin a pre-determining factor for the future. Baptism then becomes expiation of a fault, recovery from ancestral weakness, or liquidation of an evil heritage. It is hardly the beginning of a future upon which a human history worthy of the name can be based.

2. In the context of historicity, baptism becomes the foundation for positive and constructive events in the life of the baptized. Despite limits imposed by finitude and the forces of evil, the baptized are called to build up themselves, at the same time working for the edification of the entire community. The Augustinian theory focuses so one-sidedly on the "rescue" and "remedy" aspects of the sacrament that it makes baptism much more the destruction of evil than the building up of the Church.

3. Presupposed in the historicity of Christian existence is the possibility of free choice and ratification in all of life's situations. The future of Christians before God is not decided by interior or exterior forces playing with their destiny. They make decisions for themselves; in taking personal stands in the face of these forces, they respond to calls to create the future. The Augustinian theory makes people's own temporal and eternal destiny too dependent upon decisions and dispositions made apart from their own personal existence. In putting forth a mystical collectivism that defines, fixes, and determines the destinies of free beings, it reveals itself incompatible with theories emphasizing personal responsibility in historical process. People become little more than playthings in the hands of superior powers.

Nothing more clearly shows how little Augustine takes into consideration the precise point of personal freedom than his theory of conflicting servitudes. In this theory, the baptized, once freed in the sacrament from the slavery of sin, are introduced into the service of God, and all possibility of sinning is removed.[21] With some exaggeration we might characterize his thought this way: Augustine seems to condemn the redeemed to the love of God, just as he condemned the unredeemed to the service of the devil. He proposes a fearful symmetry between these two determinisms, thus eliminating in one fell swoop that marvelous adventure of liberty, where free persons make choices at each and every step on their historical journeys to fullness of life.

Similar to second-century authors like Pseudo-Barnabas, Augustine sins against historicity when he gives the sacrament of baptism an almost punctual efficacy. To say that in baptism original sin is "wiped away" in the same way that personally committed sins are forgiven gives the sacrament a function far beyond its proper limits. It does not really remain the visible sign of the dialogue between grace and faith, characterized by the pilgrimage that Christians share together. Baptism becomes nothing but the instantaneous passing from nothingness to wholeness, from sinfulness to sanctity. Such a notion is easy prey to seeing the sacrament as magic, a notion Augustine himself would have condemned with utmost severity.

4. Finally, the historicity of Christian existence demands that man be seen as a flesh-spirit unity. A Christian's personal history is never just the story of a soul. Nor is human becoming simply spiritual becoming. Body and soul we commit ourselves to the future. The Augustinian theory makes sense only by taking its

meaning from a warped idea of flesh. In maintaining that conception and birth, as biological, sexual phenomena, are carriers of moral evil, Augustine removes them from the domain of on-going creation. The act of procreation becomes more the transmission of the "aboriginal catastrophe" than the first moment in a new and personal history. Augustine's theory brings in a dualistic perspective, looking to a separation of body and soul. A more historical understanding of human beings sees them as integral units tending toward unity. Imposing such dualism on the Bible's unitary anthropology cuts the heart out of the revealed message on this particularly important point.

These reflections on Augustine's thought will close our chapter on the biblical and patristic tradition concerning baptism. We have pointed out the problem so keenly felt today of dogmatizing one or another non-historical approach to the sacrament, often precisely because the Church has not exercised a critical enough standard in receiving patristic authorities. To take Hermas, Irenaeus, and Augustine as links in an homogeneous tradition, of equal value for all times, is to ignore seriously the socio-cultural, historical conditions that have influenced all of their writings. It is to forget that they were responding to concrete questions raised in a particular epoch within a specific milieu. Their questions, moreover, are not necessarily the same as those posed today in an industrialized society.

Does this mean that we are to leave aside the entire body of patristic evidence? Not at all. But the Fathers must be read critically to unearth the principal themes of revelation that they have conveyed—themes as timely today as in their era. In this study we are attempting to show that one of these themes, so strikingly harmonious with both biblical revelation and contemporary thought, is the historical understanding of Christian existence. In our final chapter, we shall present several pressing modern problems bearing upon baptism, taking into account as fully as possible the historicity of baptismal existence.

3
Baptism and
Contemporary Problems

I
BAPTISM AND CONTEMPORARY SOCIETY

This chapter is not intended to be an "ex professo" treatment of contemporary pastoral questions such as the debate over infant baptism. Our intention is to focus in on key problems involved in contemporary baptismal theory and practice, remaining on the fundamental level of theological anthropology. To the degree that this elucidation is successful, we will have in hand the elements basic to solving the particular questions raised on the pastoral, liturgical, and pedagogical levels.

A quick over-view of the contemporary scene enables us to designate problems into two major groupings: (1) Baptism and Personal Freedom, and (2) Baptism and Consciousness of Community.

Baptism and Personal Freedom

The word freedom comes up over and over again in contemporary debates concerning baptism. Karl Barth, claiming that the practice of infant baptism violently manipulates personal freedom, has protested clearly against this practice.[22] On the other hand, Jean Daniélou, critical of postponing baptism until adolescence, took his stand against giving undue emphasis to freedom and personal commitment.[23] The question then arises: What, in contemporary thought, is meant by freedom?

First of all, freedom is seen to be bi-polar, both a capacity and a state. As a state it is revealed in the plans and goals of individuals and communities and refers to the human capacity to choose, decide, and create options. As a capacity it is exercised in selective understanding, and refers to the state of independence, autonomy, and self-determination. Contemporary thinking refuses to lock either of these dimensions of freedom into one system. Any preference for freedom as a state over freedom as a capacity, for instance, runs the danger of totalitarianism, stifling the personal capacity to be free. Systematizing the capacity to be free, so that only the personal point of view is valued, leads to anarchy.

How, then, avoid these two extremes? Only by recognizing that these two dimensions of freedom give rise to a tension irreducible to a system. By its nature this tension expresses itself in a perpetual dialectic, borne by all who desire that mankind be free. Any true community, for instance, finds both its greatness and its deepest pain in this tension. Focusing attention simultaneously on the common good and individual welfare, it offers no easy life. It considers actual problems and looks to those yet to come, taking into account both the community's and the individual's history.

Secondly, freedom is pluralistic, conditioned by

the multiple possibilities that today's society presents. Contemporary people find themselves confronted with a multitude of choices, all giving them options for realizing their autonomous "state" of freedom. The very complexity of choices reminds them of the relativity of so many principles, laws, institutions, and systems. Consequently they live in danger of falling into relativism, thereby losing all taste for absolutes. In these conditions they journey to be free. They may want to ignore the choices they do not want to make, but their only hope lies in accepting honestly the tension arising from living in a pluralistic society. They will choose to move along a particular path, but they will not refuse dialogue with those who have chosen other routes. In other words, by giving their "yes" to a particular call or vocation, they do not lose sight of what remains relative to that call-response.

Finally, freedom is secular, emancipated from any religious tutelage. Contemporary people see their freedom as a gift of nature, and they believe that their liberation depends mostly upon themselves and their peers. They see little need for the Church in solving existential questions. In case of sickness, they no longer seek a priest; they go to a physician or a therapist. If they find themselves struck by poverty, they go to the state or to social welfare organizations. Even the idea of salvation has lost its exclusively supernatural connotation; it is inter-mingled with ideas of natural happiness, including an entire array of possibilities, ranging from development of personal talents to sexual fulfillment. The capacity to be free no longer develops uniquely around goals mediated or pre-fabricated by the Church; in an ever-increasing way they are presented by people themselves. In the same way the state of being free is no longer holiness or the beatific vision. More to contemporary people's liking is a state that facilitates development of their own creativity.

II
THE THEOLOGICAL SIGNIFICANCE OF FREEDOM

Bi-polar, pluralistic, and secular contemporary, the notion of freedom must be examined theologically. This we now undertake with regard to baptism and the historicity of Christian existence.

Baptism and Freedom-as-Capacity

The first question calling for clarification is this: How does the dialectic between freedom-as-capacity and freedom-as-state find its expression in an historical understanding of baptism? If, in fact, no such expression is to be found, then baptism can no longer be understood as a free action or a freeing event. It is only another manifestation of the Church's paternalism, seeking to protect its members and force them to religious conformity. Sartre's irony would then be true: "I had been baptized, like so many others, to preserve my independence; in denying me baptism, the family would have feared it was doing violence to my soul. As a registered Catholic, I was free, I was normal. 'Later,' they said, 'he'll do as he likes.' "[24]

How, then, is baptism a free action? If we look to infant baptism, it is difficult to see how such young infants are acting freely. Even in adult baptism, fear, utilitarian self-interest, or a sense of conformity can often replace a free, well-thought-out choice as a motive for entering into the sacrament. It can be argued, of course, that in every instance where a person cannot freely present himself/herself for baptism, the community (either through his/her parents or his/her educators in the faith), can act freely in his/her name, presuming and anticipating his/her future consent. In this way traditional theology has argued that infants and others incapable of free choice are to be baptized "in the faith of the Church." Leaving aside for later discussion this difficult and important notion, we want to stress here that the freedom embodied in the sacrament is essentially a faith action. I deliberately refer to a faith action (and not an act of faith), since in the context of historicity, baptism is not something punctual and immediate, but a progressively realized action.

If we speak of an individual's baptism as an historical faith action, we refer to it as a personal response to a call from God. Like God's call, the individual's response has a past, a present, and a future.

Some may object here, cautioning that such thinking will relativize baptism so it will no longer be that irrevocable event in a person's life, accomplished once for all times and all relationships. But I am not saying that. In fact, this baptismal "faith action" so enters into the individual's temporal and relational history that it becomes integral to his/her life process. As a crucial moment in that total process, it is never to be revoked arbitrarily.

Essential to the sacrament in this perspective are the Church's relational and temporal dimensions. Temporal history as pilgrimage and relational history as dialogue clarify it. Together they give baptism its meaning.

The sacrament then is to be celebrated only at a time when God's call in the Church is present to the individual in an historically valid way. Those responsible for a child's future, for instance, recognize that baptism can take place before catechesis, so long as the continuity between the moment of baptism and the subsequent life of faith has a serious chance of success. In the practice of confirmation, the Church has attempted to assure this continuity by extending the baptismal faith-action in two sacramental moments: baptism and confirmation. Confirmation does indeed "confirm" the believer's "post factum" ratifying of his baptismal commitment. God's Spirit, in this perspective, validates baptism when freely received by the believer. The testimony of the Acts of the Apostles gives to this practice its indispensable theological basis.

It is possible that in new situations the baptismal faith-action will continue to be shaped in still other ways. We need only cite the recent experiment in the diocese of Arras, in northern France, where baptism was deferred until the age of reason and confirmation until the age of twenty.[25] It is within reason to predict that the time for the sacrament's celebration will be extended more and more as baptism undergoes even other changes determined by the ecclesial and missionary situation of various regions.

These technical matters are not, of course, the heart of the baptismal question. What remains essential is that baptism, at whatever chronological moment it is celebrated, at some point must be ratified freely by the persons baptized. In no way can this be done for them vicariously. Otherwise the sacrament is no longer a personal, free action. It may have transformed them into children of God or incorporated them into an ecclesial

flock, but it has not served to advance them into adulthood where they can make their own decisions or commit themselves to a pilgrim Church.

Baptism and Freedom-as-State

Baptism is not only concerned, however, with the
individual's right and capacity to choose; it also serves
freedom-as-state, leading the Church to a kind of existence in which a true pilgrimage toward self-determination and self-realization can be undertaken. In traditional theological terms, baptism leads to salvation. In
speaking of salvation are we talking only about celestial
beatitude and its foretaste in sanctifying grace? Or can
we also speak of man's fulfillment and his progressive
self-actualization? Is salvation people's divinization by
their submission to divine power? Or is it their humani-
zation by their freely chosen relationship to their God?

How we answer the question of salvation will condition our notion of baptism as a factor in leading to
freedom-as-state. Contemporary theology has already
furnished some elements in answering this question,
and these we must now investigate.

First of all, the idea of salvation (and with it baptism) is being freed from its "hamartiological hyp-
nosis." Baptism is not seen to be simply the washing
away of original or personally committed sin; it is more
a critical moment in a person's total historical fulfillment. Its grace, therefore, is not so much the healing
and reparation of sin as God's gift of himself so that
the baptized can become who they really and totally
are. Certainly God's gift of himself is much more than
an antidote against personal sins. God enters into

human history to overcome all of humanity's alien-
ations, whether they can be personally faulted or not.
Even the transcendence of God is less a metaphysical
and static state and more an historical and dynamic
movement, going beyond what has been and is to what
will be. Within human history God makes real his own
history, creatively acting to bring about his kingdom
among people. Bonhoeffer put it this way: "God's transcendence is made real in our cities and in our
towns."[26]

To view salvation as fulfillment harmonizes with
contemporary ideas about freedom. If baptism, an
entry into freedom, is the first step toward a higher
degree of responsibility and self-worth, we can say that
the baptized are indeed called to be adults, ready to
take up their responsibilities and enter into the adventure of on-going creation. The sacrament then truly
leads to freedom-as-state even though experience tells
us that this state of freedom is often not attained. How
many Christians, for instance, seeing their baptism as
little more than capital security for eternity, choose as
little as possible! This oft-ingrained misunderstanding
of the sacrament has led Church authorities to refuse or
postpone baptism in certain situations, for the sacrament must be an integration of the tension between
freedom-as-capacity and freedom-as-state, or it is not a
sacrament at all.

Baptism, therefore, marks the beginning of the
Christian's dialectical, historical journey. Because of
people's propensity to opt against freedom (or not to
choose at all), education for freedom becomes a baptismal urgency. Without such education, one dimension of
freedom will annihilate the other. There is no optimum
age for this education, just as there is no optimum age

for baptism. Some persons in their forties are so minimally free that any responsible pastor would hesitate to baptize them. On the other hand, some children manifest at a very young age an intuitive understanding of their own baptismal history, already translated into action. What is important to remember is that the chronological moment for baptism is much less important than the sacrament's meaning and significance as a faith-action contexted in a history of past freedom received, present freedom lived, and future freedom to be created.

The Character of Baptism

Before concluding this section on the relationships between the two notions of freedom and the significance of baptism, it will be useful to study briefly the notion of the "character" of the sacrament. Contemporary theology has set to work to demythologize this notion of "character." It is not a quantity automatically added to people's spiritual substance whether they are aware of it or not. Rather, "character" refers to baptism's stability and permanence as rooted in God's promise and plan. In baptism believers acquire a steadfastness in their pilgrimage with their peers toward fulfillment in God. However, their stability does not come from themselves, but from God's fidelity to his promise and his choosing to realize his plan of salvation. God's stability gives the baptized the real possibility of sharing in the history of Jesus, as St. Paul indicated when he spoke of Christians as new creatures, baptized into Christ to walk in a newness of life (Rom. 6:4).

This permanence, moreover, belongs to both the

order of being and the order of action. To be "con-
figured" to Christ in baptism means that Christians
share in his dignity; they are called to take in who Jesus
is and what he has done. From this participation in
Jesus' own history, Christians harmonize their own actions with his. Their pilgrimage may undergo radical
changes in the course of a lifetime, but they remain fundamentally linked to God's plan; the influence of Jesus
on their lives has a permanent and stable quality that
continues with them.

God's plan, however, is not a stereotyped blueprint
for a pre-fabricated existence! Continuity in Christ is
profoundly historical, harmonious with all the changes
implied in freedom-as-capacity working toward freedom-as-state. Baptism indicates that God's permanent
and stable freedom constantly dialogues with man's
growing, journeying freedom. The sacrament does not
guarantee that Christians will always retain their likeness to Christ; they may in fact renounce their baptismal incorporation into his life and history. Yet, the permanence of God's plan in Christ remains intact.

In their pilgrimage in Christ the baptized find that
God's plan for temporal and relational living gives a
permanent and definitive orientation to their lives. Baptism is their moment of focusing in on that plan. To
speak of the sacramental "character" as an indelible
mark rooted in the human soul does not harmonize
with man's nature as personal, free, and historical. The
sacrament's permanence is to be found only in God.[27]

Baptism and Pluralism

Baptism, a faith action conditioned by the tensions

inherent in living out freedom historically, is also influenced by today's pluralistic society. A mere glance at today's world uncovers an immense variety of philosophies, theologies, and methods of salvation. Each has its particular nuance in offering self-fulfillment, unity, and happiness. Contemporary people find themselves bombarded by different religions, all competing for their allegiance. The Catholic Church, to say nothing of Christianity itself, rarely predominates in an explicit way, although the Christian heritage often is found hidden in the great stream of modern ideas, be they existentialist, Marxist, or facist. As we have already pointed out, the historical understanding of human existence is of Judaeo-Christian origin. Because, however, its presence is so often diffused and hidden, Christianity is no longer the sole spokesperson for salvation. It is part of the contemporary pluralistic scene and must compete on an equal footing with other currents of thought and plans of action. Liberty, equality, and fraternity, for example, are not simply Christian values today; they are received in a laicized form, attributed partly to the Enlightenment and partly to the French Revolution.

The Catholic Church (to say nothing of the other Christian churches) has taken steps to respond to this pluralistic situation even in its theological formulations. The old axiom "Outside of the church no salvation" has been so highly nuanced that it has been replaced, really, by a more ecumenical and irenic approach to other journeys of faith. Catholic theologians today have come to admit that salvation is just as possible outside of the Catholic Church as within it. Karl Rahner's theory of the "anonymous Christian" is characteristic in this regard.[28] Rahner considers as "anonymous Christians" all those who take the human situation seriously and strive for love and justice, whether they accept belief in God or not. In fact, there are indications that Rahner had certain neo-Marxists in mind in elaborating this theory.

Just how does this pluralistic situation condition the baptized and candidates for baptism in their freedom of choice? Are they condemned to indecision? Must they become multi-lateral, choosing options one after the other, some complementary, others contradictory? Are Christians and catechumens, recognizing the multiplicity of truths and ways to be true, forced to a relativism in determining which are worth considering? The decline of the old-fashioned missionary spirit and the rise of the spirit of partnership seem to indicate that this is the case. Certainly in some Christian circles, criticism, struggle, and revolution in the spirit of the Gospel are more popular ideals than the mission of making all peoples Christian! An enormous yearning for solidarity with the world's oppressed and with non-Christian artisans of a better world helps form the identity crisis that Christians face today. Is Christianity simply irrelevant dogma? If not, what does it have to offer to contemporary, pluralistic man?

The first element in any response to these questions is that Christian freedom and identity, although in a state of crisis, remains a *believer's* freedom and identity. By the very fact that their belief is in Christ, Christians are oriented toward an absolute and determined goal. To believe in Jesus (or, to use Paul's language, to believe *toward* him and by reference to him) is to admit with one's entire being that Jesus is the way, the truth, and the life. Belief in Jesus saves the believer because faith gives the believer's own history its unity and fundamental orientation. Believers know toward which center they incessantly direct their life; in all their choices they absorb the history of Jesus into their own. As the central focus of a Christian's belief, Jesus as Christ and Lord does not lurk in the shadows of relativity. Jesus admits of no other absolute and demands that each Christian serve only one master. To stretch this point or put it to the test is to contradict the very essence of belief.

Christian believers today, however, know that this faith is in crisis. Even if they hold to its foundation in Jesus, they do not always know how to build upon that foundation, for faith's absolute focus co-exists with so many relative focal points. The distinction traditional in theology between Jesus and the Church as focal points of belief remains even more relevant today. The Latin text of the Creed makes this distinction even clearer; Latin syntax refers to "believing *in* God" or "*in* Christ," but never to "believing *in* the Church." The preposition "in" makes all the difference. Its presence indicates commitment to an absolute; its absence indicates commitment to a person or society relative to an absolute. This second manner of believing lies behind Vatican II's speaking of a "hierarchy of truths."[29] We do not, therefore, believe the Church in the same manner as we believe *in* God or *in* Jesus.

Correlative to this pluralism in the domain of faith is a similar phenomenon in the realm of ethics. We touch upon this parallel to mention two areas important to our study. First, just as there is in the domain of dogma a "hierarchy of truths," so in the domain of ethics is there a "hierarchy of commandments." In their baptismal faith action, Christians must remember that God's love for people and the love of people for

one another and for themselves is the summit around
which all other moral behavior is relative. Secondly, a
pluralistic view of the baptismal commitment teaches
Christians to respect the seriousness of ethical attitudes
found in other religions and systems of salvation.

Obviously the relationship between the absolute
and the relative posed by a pluralistic society impacts
the believer's freedom. Christians must live to the full
the dialectical tension that this impact brings. Remem-
bering that Jesus remains the absolute focus of their
faith, Christians must nevertheless pay serious attention
to all that is relative to their fundamental commitment.
Christian faith, for instance, confesses that all human
values take their meaning from their relationship to the
God manifest in Jesus. Tertullian spoke of the "catho-
licity of God," indicating that God, in his uniqueness,
remains universally open to all existence relative to
him.[30] Christian freedom, always taking what is relative
as seriously as does God himself, constantly reshapes
the dialectic between the absolute and the relative. This
reshaping, so essential in meeting the crisis of relativism posed by a pluralistic society, means that Christians remain open to change. They continue to be baptized only "in" Christ and refuse to accept as absolute
anything human, even Church structures, doctrines, and
laws. In the midst of accepting diversity, they maintain
that God alone, made flesh in Jesus the Christ and
Lord, is absolute.

What will this centered, yet multi-faceted existence
produce, if not new possibilities for realizing personal
and communal historicity? Thanks to the tensions of
pluralistic living, Christians find themselves stimulated
to new levels of creativity. But they can also discover
themselves overwhelmed and dismayed—more and
more alienated—by the sheer vastness of options. It is

precisely this choice between alienation and creation that faces all the baptized in today's historical, dialectical world. How this choice is made will determine the quality of the baptismal faith-action in modern times.

Baptism and Secularization

We now want to consider contemporary society's secular dimension to see its influence on baptismal freedom. Taking as our starting point the "Kingdom-Church-world" triptych, we see that the Gospels place the Church between the Kingdom and the world. The baptized, in their turn, mediate between the Kingdom and the era in which they live.

Among the oldest baptismal texts in the Scriptures we find the notion that by baptismal faith Christians "enter the Kingdom" or "see the Kingdom." By the "Kingdom" the Scriptures refer to man's existential condition—a definitive relationship to God that is incomplete but tending to a fullness of truth, justice, and love. The New Testament goes on to say that this "Kingdom is not of this world," meaning that in its origin and fullness it is not to be identified with any given secular society. Catholic theology in the past, tending to over-emphasize this distinction between the Kingdom and the world, practically equated the Kingdom and the Church, giving the Church superiority and transcendence over the world! Such theology prompted an ethic of separation and betrayed the New Testament's fundamentally historical and incarnate character. The Church is not the Kingdom, nor does it stand over against the world. Both Church and world have their destiny in the Kingdom.

The Church's role in this triptych is ministerial.

Standing between the Kingdom and the world, it serves as mediator to transfigure the world into a Kingdom of truth, justice, and love. Often this ministry has been tainted with paternalistic and maternalistic tendencies. But the Church is not the world's nourishing mother nor its protective father. Church and world are partners in salvation. They work together to build up the Kingdom fulfilled and unified. Christians build up the Kingdom by injecting their own charisms into their professional, social, and familial activities. Living in partnership with the secular world, they cooperate and share freedom in working together to bring both Church and world to the fullness of the Kingdom.

III
EXISTENCE IN COMMUNITY AND BAPTISM

The departure point for all our reflections in this study has been our thesis that baptism is a focal point in the midst of a total historical process. The entire process (which we have called historicity) gives baptism its power. Without this intimate connection to a community's history, baptism would be no more than a pure formality or senseless ritual, with no point of reference beyond an immediate person in an immediate place. As it is, however, the community was present at the sacrament's origins and remains present to its final purpose.

In other words, persons become Christians by a community and for that community. They receive the sacrament from the community that is theirs either by birth or by choice, and they are then called to help build up that community. Baptism's horizons, then, are clearly communal. This perception of the sacrament, drawn fundamentally from the New Testament and the Fathers of the Church, enables us to relate baptismal theology to the contemporary anthropological theories we have already mentioned. With the personalists we maintain that this historical process of communal incorporation takes place through a series of "I-Thou" encounters. Christians find their own histories raised to consciousness and actualized in a series of personal give-and-take situations. Given certain reservations, we can also borrow from the Marxists their perspective that man is a totality of social relationships, a living concretization of the society to which he belongs. Who can deny, for instance, that a baptized child's formation takes place in a given sociological and cultural situation? Societal classes, together with regional and national mentalities and prejudices, influence a child, Baptismal histories, therefore, will vary—the child of a migrant worker will have a different personal history than a university professor's child. But each will have his or her contribution to the community's total life.

The Community in Its Relationship to the Baptized

1. The Faith of the Church

Considerable confusion has arisen from baptism administered in "the faith of the Church." Some see such baptizing as only another instance of authoritarianism, a sort of piracy enabling the Church to acquire new members without so much as one word of explanation beforehand. Others view the "faith of the Church" as an established doctrinal system foisted upon all the baptized so that no subsequent action is

necessary to explain why this system is best for salvation. Still others feel that this type of faith is not so
much a doctrinal system as simply the living conviction
of concerned Church members whose belief makes up
for what is lacking in the person to be baptized.

The contemporary notions of freedom that we
have already considered react against such ideas. No
one, it is asserted, can believe for somebody else. A father cannot believe for his son, nor a son for his father.
Faith is not a liquid to be poured from vessel to vessel,
but an existential action so personal to each believer
that each must live out his or her own faith response. In
the days of patriarchal systems, it was normal and accepted that the father would commit his entire family
to Christ when he made his own commitment. In the
Middle Ages, when a more matriarchal attitude pre-
vailed, it was easy to accept a Mother Church giving
birth to whomsoever she pleased. Careful to inculcate
all the truths she communicated to her children in baptism, she could then burn all who refused that truth.
Even though the Inquisition as such has disappeared,
the formal principle of baptizing in the "faith of the
Church" remains the same as in the Middle Ages—a
community's faith substitutes for a person's faith. How,
then, do we avoid doing violence to personal freedom in
baptizing in this way?

First of all, it is important to keep in mind the
theological distinction between faith as what we believe
(fides quae creditur) and faith by which we believe
(fides qua creditur). Unless we are attentive to the difference between the doctrinal content we profess to believe and the act of professing belief, we will be locked
in a hopeless impasse.

Of these two manners of faith, the second, the action of believing, is primordial. (Only an exaggerated intellectualism gives priority to the formulated content of belief.) Historically the first disciples' "yes" to Jesus was their action of believing. Enabling them to see Jesus as the Christ, it preceded any definitive ecclesial creed. Before there was a Church, therefore, there was faith in Jesus. This first faith-action was not primarily the disciple's intellectual conviction that Jesus' teachings were true; it was more their intuitive conviction that Jesus was himself genuine and true—that in his life, words, and deeds he was faithful to who and what he was. The disciples sensed that in his truest self Jesus responded as a man in union with God. This response the disciples took as their own. As Walter Kasper has put it: "It is not a question of intellectual understanding of particular points, but of certitude about the totality."[31]

Faith as the action of believing is historical faith; it is the believer's freedom historically directed to Jesus; in this aspect of faith Christians blend their own histories with that of Jesus. Its priority in the total faith action does not imply, however, that the doctrinal content of faith is of only negligible importance. The creeds and defined dogmas are the stuff around which catechesis is built, and they give direction to the faith choices a Christian must make. If we give the priority to the creeds and dogmas, however, we run the risk of reducing faith to sheer intellectual assent, and faith becomes more an ideology than an historical journey.

When we speak of baptism in the "faith of the Church," therefore, we refer first of all to the total historical action in which faith is brought about. This action of believing is not without its doctrinal content; its declared norms give direction and light. What remains primary, however, is the historical pilgrimage on the part of the persons who make up the community into which the person is baptized, be that person a child or adult.

This faith action, to be fully effective, must be communicative, planned, and responsible.

As communicative, the faith of the Church is an on-going dialogue with the living, personal God. Faith, like any true act of love, implies relationship and shared life. When persons love, they choose to give themselves to one another; their love flows into a communication leading them to a world beyond themselves. In an analogous manner, the faith of the Church has its dimension of "going beyond." Such faith, convinced of the good that God in Jesus has brought to all mankind, encourages the Church to share that good with all persons born into the world.

To be truly communicative, however, a believing Church does not seek to impose its life in a possessive way. Communicative faith invites, it does not possess. A truly faithful Church, therefore, invites free persons to become who they are. Just as God, in his gift of himself in grace, anticipates the human person's free response, so the Church, in communicating its faith to persons to be baptized, looks forward to their freedom. Pledging itself to these persons and their historical journey, it respects them as free. In baptizing their children, Christian parents affirm their own children's freedom and become ministers of God's anticipatory grace. Faith as communicative, therefore, respects historicity and encourages baptismal freedom.

As planned, the faith of the Church is not simply an on-the-spot communication of its own richness and dynamism. Because it looks to human persons as historical, the Church must be cautious about entering into faith relationships without sufficient concern for their future. Only those persons are to be baptized in whom there is a serious possibility for the development of Christian freedom. Such a possibility, of course, includes the inevitable risk that the faith-life offered in baptism may be modified, criticized, or even refused. But such is the realism of baptism as a planned faith action in the total journey of a believing Church toward its God.

Finally, the faith of the Church is responsible. In baptism, the Church takes a stand with regard to God, the world, and its own conscience. In baptizing a child, for instance, the community of believers declares itself ready to share in all the conflicts, confrontations, and crises that may follow in that child's life. Children grow and develop only because the community foresaw their coming and continues to surround and influence them. If children are to reveal themselves to this community, they must first have this community revealed to them. Only then can they begin to accept themselves as free persons, with their own journey to live. They may, of course, choose a path that will lead them away from the community that baptized them. In a very real sense, therefore, infant baptism is a wager, and in some family circumstances the Church's most responsible action may be to defer baptism until the child can appreciate its significance and implications. What is important is that responsible free action be preserved in both the Church and the person being baptized.

By understanding the "faith of the Church" as communicative, planned, and responsible, we see that baptism cannot be some mystical entity into which the initiates are plunged. Baptizing individuals in the faith of the Church does not mean imposing a doctrinal system to preserve them from heresy. Nor does it mean drafting them into an army where they no longer choose for themselves. Baptism in the faith of the Church must be entry into free, historical living. If it is not a participation in the successes and failures of the Church, it is no longer the sacrament of Christian historicity.

This brings us to a word on an important pastoral problem. Pastoral experience indicates that in some family instances the Church's most responsible action may be the deferring of baptism. What, for instance, of marginal, indifferent, "non-practicing" Christians who present their children for baptism? An alert pastor knows there will be little follow-up in such circumstances. The family's faith is often so diminished or malformed that anything taught to the children in catechism will be ignored or contradicted in the home. How, in such circumstances, does the "faith of the Church" enter the scene? And how is it possible to judge the family's "Christian-ness"? A catechism examination would be ridiculous, giving undue emphasis to the content of faith rather than to the action of believing. Nor can we look only at the "practice" of religion. For faith, since it concerns a person's entire existential orientation, cannot be measured simply by cultic norms. Nor do we want to fall into that psychologically and ethically primitive state of refusing baptism on so-called moral grounds—refusing, for instance, to baptize children born out of wedlock.

An appropriate solution to this problem can be found in the pastoral stance taken in the large urbanized areas of France. The pioneers in this area have been the priests of the "Mission de France."[32] Their basic approach has been one of on-going dialogue between priest and parents to help the parents to clarify their own faith and their motives for wanting to baptize their children. What is avoided is any unilateral refusal to baptize; the decision for or against baptism is reached in common. Since the process of dialogue extends over a certain period of time, it is also necessary to extend the different stages in the baptismal process: the inscription, the dialogue, and finally the baptismal celebrations. Even after baptism an intense collaboration continues between the parents and the pastor. (The documents of the French hierarchy indicate that the idea of unbaptized children dying in a state of original sin is no longer the burning pastoral issue it once was. Children who die while inscribed on the rolls for baptism are to be given Christian burial.)

It is not our intention here to go into all the details of this pastoral problem. We wish only to underscore how harmoniously this pastoral practice of deferring baptism blends with the historical notion of Christian existence. Both temporal and relational historicity come to life in this approach to the sacrament, so marked by the idea that baptism proclaims Christian existence as a living pilgrimage embracing the entirety of a person's life. No longer need the Church feel that it is baptizing people to drag them into some pious abstraction or legalistic generality. The sacrament, when faithfully translating Christianity as historical, looks to the Christian life as a maturing awareness, including times of belief and disbelief. In baptizing in its own faith, the Church asks new members to take seriously their own pilgrimage together with its own.

2. The Role of Parents in "Socialization"

Although this theme belongs properly to the psychologist, the sociologist, and the educator, we want to gather together a few elements basic to religious sociology to consider what bearing they have on the notion of baptism in the "faith of the Church."

Religious sociology, observing the diverse and complex social relationships in persons and groups, speaks to religious "behavior." Content to describe these behavioral phenomena and to portray their interdependence, it does not pretend to investigate ultimate goals or inner motivations. From a strictly sociological point of view Christianity can be categorized together with the other world religions. What this categorization does not take into account, however, is the distinction in contemporary theology between religion and faith. To refer to Christianity as a religion necessarily accentuates its system of salvation: dogmas, laws, and institutions. To look first of all at Christianity's faith, however, is to see what differentiates it most profoundly from other salvific ways. Religious sociology does not make judgments concerning religious faith as such. Consequently, to view Christianity simply from a sociological perspective does not take into account the baptized in their personal or communal historicity, be that temporal or relational.

Keeping in mind the boundaries proper to a sociological approach to Christianity, we turn now to the important perspective that religious sociology brings to an understanding of baptism: the notion of "socialization." We mean by this the act of placing individual goods in common and attributing them to the community.[33] Applied to individuals this notion refers to a person's progressive integration into a given society. Through the process of "socialization" individual persons take their place in a given society. They become "at home" in their sociological milieu, free to live out their roles without feeling alienated.

In contemporary society individual persons find themselves integrated into many societies at once. So, too, the baptized find themselves living in many worlds simultaneously. Children, for instance, belong to their families, schools, or other extra-familial educational groups; adults, in turn, must reckon with their professional worlds, the political arena, the Church, and all their sexual relationships. All are societal relationships, and all involve the person in the phenomenon of socialization.

I mention sexuality as a separate societal grouping because of its bearing upon baptismal theology. Each baptized person must integrate into the society of his or her own sex, always taking into account the complementary sexual grouping. Can we declare at the moment of baptism that a person is a son or daughter of God and then remain in prudish silence about the importance that sexuality will play in the person's subsequent history as a Christian? Must we not continue to be aware of the implications that the convergence and the complementarity of the sexes has on the theology of the sacrament?

For the baptized to be integrated sexually into the Christian community there must be "bearers of socialization" in the sexual sphere. A society's anonymous factors—its laws and institutions—can never succeed by themselves at integrating individual persons into a societal group. If a person is to become an integral part of the faith community on the sexual level, he must be in contact with bearers of the heritage, themselves consciously personalist in responding to the sexual growth and development.

Here, of course, parents play a particularly important role. Without falling into the delusion that all parents are born educators, the exigency remains: if children are to be integrated into the community of faith on any level, the task falls immediately upon the parents. What we have said about baptism and freedom has its bearing here. The historical character of the sacrament puts demands on parents to adopt as wide a perspective as possible in their children's religious upbringing. Otherwise they will scarcely be able to enter into effective, expanding, and harmonious socialization. Sexually, for instance, they will grow up repressed and ill-formed for living as sexual adults in the Christian community.

The question is wider, of course, than its sexual components. From an historical perspective education for integration into society does not begin when a child is born. It begins in the lives of the ancestors. Their own education conditions their abilities to be "bearers of socialization." If they themselves have not been trained adequately, they will hardly be able to develop their own children's interests and capacities. The wise parent knows that the child in front of him is both child and future adult, and he presents to the child the measure of responsibility appropriate to his age, aware that careful progress can lead to surprising results. The child receiving an education sensitive to his own historicity grows to be an adult capable of bearing socialization to his or her own progeny. Historically slanted education is crucial if children are to grow into responsible adulthood.

Finally, I want to add one theological observation which may seem surprising to some readers. Recognizing that the spirit of baptism is the spirit of the cross, the entire educative process related to baptism will be marked by the cross. Taking up the cross means embracing the world as it is, with all its ambivalence. The spirit of the cross, identified with neither optimism nor pessimism, calls for a realistic attitude in accepting crisis and conflict as normal phenomena in creating the future. At the very least it strives to make what is imperfect and faulty a little less so. Without the cross, Christian living often substitutes a facile naiveté for charity. Well-grounded charity does not love everything, nor does it pretend to.

Charity is not some sort of tepid sauce poured over every aspect of existence. At times in our history this kind of false charity has invaded ecclesial domains, but it is neither Christian nor evangelical. The Gospel message demands that evil be opposed, not covered over. The Sermon on the Mount is a critical message, recognizing opposition in the world as normal. It proposes a Gospel dialectic that is both a "yes" and a "no" in response to various aspects of human historicity. Because conflict is built into humanity, the Gospel tells us to face it with options, assenting to this, dissenting from that. Neither "yes" nor "no" responses to existence are predetermined as good or evil.

Consequently, education related to baptism must instill this spirit of the cross. Educated in this fashion, Christians will be able to accept the dialectic between good and evil with all the conflict and crisis that true progress demands. In no other spirit can socialization be achieved, either personally or communally. What the cross brings is critical charity, able to protest against injustice and disorder. Charity, in the spirit of the Gospel, lives with diversity and works to promote harmony as divergent peoples and groups move in their journeys through life.

The Baptized in Their Relationship to the Community

If the Christian community gives direction, purpose, and communal historicity to the individual in baptism, it remains equally true that the individual's participation in the sacrament gives strength and direction to the community. Christians in baptism are called to build up the community, and each one brings his or her own charism to that task.

We have already spoken of the family as a focal point of baptismal action. Now we must move to that larger ecclesial community, the parish. Recent sociological developments are calling into question even this traditional form of community, and we want to turn now to examine from a contemporary perspective the community into which Christians are baptized.

1. True Community and the Parish

Urbanization, the first factor to consider in examining the parish, has marked the end of the rural type of life at the base of traditional parish structure. This rural situation, with its homogeneous groups, favoring mutual acquaintance and a regular rhythm of life, was such a strong force sociologically that it was able to move into the cities rather easily. Relatively autonomous parish groups could exist side by side without disturbing or even influencing one another. Today, however, such communities are disappearing rapidly. Even in rural areas in some countries, parochial structures have atrophied to the point of death. Thanks to the phenomenon of de-Christianization, some of the vast medieval churches dotting the European countryside are almost empty except for a few hardy souls gathered for baptisms, weddings, and funerals. They stand as last vestiges of a once prosperous cultic artistry.

On the urban scene the emptiness is less obvious. Despite the break-up of homogeneous societal patterns, churches in large urban concentrations are often filled, and parish priests have more than enough to do. What often happens, however, is not cultic artistry. Parishes, no longer serving homogeneous groups, become sacramental factories producing goods for the religious consumer. For many Christians this parochial form is inadequate. As an example we cite the suburban "bedroom" community. People dwelling in these communities often come from other parts of the country; they have no particular roots where they live, and their jobs often necessitate frequent changes from city to city. Their lives heavily stamped with mobility, they experience a certain insecurity peculiar to contemporary "technological nomads" and lose interest in their vocation to build up a Christian community. In this overcharged situation, a certain amount of heroism is demanded to devote weekends to church activities or even to plan for Sunday Mass.

Obviously, this situation poses problems for the historicity involved in an individual's relationship to the community. How, for instance, will Christians want to see themselves as pilgrims marching with a pilgrim

Church when their entire lives are a rat-race against the clock? What does it mean to be a healthy, well-integrated, functioning member of a Church body when people's lives are constantly being uprooted or poured from one pot to another? How can local parish churches mean anything to persons whose neighborhood has little to do with their social or work lives? How, then, do Christians build up community in these circumstances?

First of all, the very mobility of contemporary society has its influence on Church structure. No longer seeing itself as a static hierarchy emphasizing an unchangeable difference between clergy and laity, Church structure today seeks to be more supple. In this perspective, coordination replaces subordination. Christians seek to create within the community convergent functions, not hierarchical grades. In building up the Church, they work to create a center to coordinate each member's charisms, seeking to preserve basic differences, yet helping each one to complement the other.

Together with increased mobility, a new call for authenticity has arisen within the Church. Young people especially do not look so much to the stability of the community's life as to its intensity. If there is stability to be found, they maintain, it must be rooted in the intensity of the group commitment.

Many contemporary Christians wonder what kind of community will meet their needs. Obviously the parish that continues to function as a true community will be attractive to such believers. Once a parish is beyond repair, however, they will not hesitate to invest their energies elsewhere. In that situation, Christians may well leave strictly geographical groupings and move toward other ways of gathering more central to their lives.

Ecclesial communities have already emerged based on the enthusiasm, spontaneity, and emphasis on affinity found in the commune movement among the young. These groupings, even among weary "bedroom" community dwellers, create an inspiring atmosphere of fervor and authenticity. The simple fact that in worship those who share the Eucharist know each other often helps to free surprising energies. In these smaller groupings lies at least one way for the Church to reconstruct a viable base of operation and recover some of the freshness that attracted so many people in the days immediately following Vatican II.

Part of the Church's mission, in fact, is to preserve these newer ecclesial forms from their inherent danger toward sectarianism. Today, as always, it is a matter of life and death for the Church to preserve unity in the midst of plurality. To the extent that a multitude of smaller, homogeneous groups represents diversity playing against unity, the Church's very life is seriously threatened. St. Paul saw this same danger in the Church in Corinth. If these smaller groupings lose the broader perspective of responsibility to the whole world involved in the entire Church's historical pilgrimage, they will unleash destructive, divisive energies, no matter how strongly they emphasize within themselves a life of shared truth and mutual charity.

The task of reconciling the old with the new falls into four major categories: (1) relationships of historical complementarity must be established between those structures of the past still active and the structures of the future; (2) newer forms of community must continue to create bonds among themselves aimed at a specifically ecclesial federation; (3) communal movements, with all their confusion, must be welcomed in recognition of their truly prophetic strains; (4) the universal perspective common to many secular youth movements must be more and more incorporated into ecclesial structures.

The blending of the old with the new, finally, belongs to priests and laity alike, for all the baptized are called to that future-oriented, eminently historical task of building up the Church. The New Testament indicates that all Christians share in the same mission and the same priesthood. We must now investigate two important scriptural notions essential to our theology of baptism: apostolate and "royal priesthood."

2. Apostolate and "Royal Priesthood"

In speaking of the apostolate, we must look first of all to the mission given to the baptized today and examine its relationship to the mission given to the apostles in New Testament literature.[34] The pertinent text is found in Matthew: "Go therefore and make disciples of all nations, baptizing them in the name of the Father and of the Son and of the Holy Spirit, teaching them to observe all that I have commanded you" (Mt. 28:19-20). Just as believers contemporary with Jesus espoused his history as their own and went out to make disciples in a non-Christian world, so baptized persons today are called to embrace that same history and form disciples in a secular society. Baptism, therefore, serves as a sending forth, encouraging believers to enter into the various factors of secular life.

As missioned disciples, however, Christians are neither messengers of the ready-made response nor proponents of law and ritual observance. Their role is more subtle. They observe the mental, spiritual, and intellectual conditions of society and respond in a language that can be understood. Apostleship, therefore, involves both receiving and giving. The Christian interprets society, and society in turn shapes and forms the Christian's message.

In contacting a society hallmarked by secularism and plurality, Christians meet a world that will not ordinarily understand the language of the catechisms and the creeds. Believers cannot expect immediate understanding of phrases like "Creator of heaven and earth," "conceived of the Holy Spirit," or "resurrection of the body." The difficult task of translating the meaning of these theological phrases is part of the Christian's apostolic vocation.

The baptized, therefore, work at a hermeneutical task. Their apostolate means being present to society so that they can understand its religious needs. Charity and the witness of a good life are not enough for a fully developed apostolic presence. Also needed are explanations and reasons for belief. It is not enough to appeal simply to the "mystery of faith."

To be effective in their apostolic calling, therefore, Christians need more than a basic catechism formation. They need to deepen their faith awareness and re-examine their expressions of belief in a world where constant search is the thinking man's bread. On-going catechesis and theology are now essential components in any Christian's baptismal history. Trained lay catechists and lay theologians assume a growing importance in the Church's apostolate. Enmeshed in the secular society in their daily lives, they acquire a sensitivity enabling them to recognize the valid points of contact between that society and the Christian message.

Excellent precedent exists for the laity taking an ever increasing role in the apostolate of theological reflection and prophetic interpretation of the Gospel message. In the early days of Christianity laypersons like Justin Martyr, Tertullian, and Origen played roles of capital importance in the Church's dialogue with society. Even in the Scriptures the links between God's work and specific cultures were forged by shepherds like Amos, physicians like Luke, and even a tax collector named Matthew!

The apostolate, therefore, remains the work of all the baptized. In reaching out to secular society, both clergy and laity act together as interpreters of the Gospel message, constantly seeking a deeper understanding of their faith. Because of their share in the Church's apostolic character, they dialogue with society to discover the truth that the Church has for the world and the world for the Church.[35]

3. The Royal Priesthood of the Faithful

Contemporary baptismal theology must also examine the scriptural notion of the "royal priesthood of the faithful." Not by accident, however, did we consider first the apostolic dimension of baptism. Had we begun by stressing the Church as more a sacerdotal corporation than an apostolic mission, we would have reversed priorities. We believe that the basis for all the Church's activity, including liturgy and worship, must be its apostolic character. If its dialogue and efforts to reach out are but prolongations of a fundamentally cultic mind-set, then the Church goes against the grain of the Gospel. Christians perform good works merely to complete what is lacking in worship and cultic ritual; they do not take the world seriously. Jesus, after all, did not found another Qumran monastery where his disciples were to pray and offer sacrifice before turning to the world. He sent his disciples out on the roadways of Galilee and Judea, insisting that they speak to the people and take their problems seriously. Prayer and worship were to be formed "on the way." The Church's fundamental structure, therefore, is not the cultic reality of the "priesthood of the faithful," but its ministry of apostolic service. Yet, in the history of Christianity this "priestly" notion has undergone many interpretations.

At the time it served as a basis for Luther's Protestant Reformation. Today, theologians have again found interest in this ancient notion. Hans Küng, for instance, has interpreted it to refer to a theology of "direct access to God."[36]

Despite his important contribution to contemporary theology, Küng has not, in my opinion, given us a particularly good commentary on "royal priesthood" and has missed the fundamental purpose behind the New Testament use of the "priestly" analogy as presented, for instance, in 1 Peter. This letter does not speak directly to the believer's immediate and intimate relationship with God. Writing to persecuted Christians dispersed throughout Asia Minor, the author's concern is solidarity within the Church. Far from supporting individual freedom over against subservient obedience to ecclesiastical authorities, he preaches unity around both Christ, the "shepherd and guardian of your souls" (1 Pet. 2:25) and the presbyters who "tend the flock of God" (1 Pet. 5:2). In this context he compares the Christian community to a "spiritual house built of living stones" (1 Pet. 2:5). The Church becomes God's "royal residence" and his "body of priests" (1 Pet. 2:9).

These last two images come from a Greek formula no longer translated as "royal priesthood," but as two terms: "royal residence" and "body of priests."[37] Rooted in Old Testament thought, these images have special reference to the Septuagint translation of the celebrated text in Exodus: "Now therefore if you will obey my voice and keep my covenant you shall be my own possession among all peoples; for all the earth is mine, and you shall be to me a kingdom of priests and a holy nation" (Ex. 19:5-6). This translation, by placing the image of "royal residence" and "body of priests" in the context of a covenant for all peoples, blends remarkably well with the "apostolic" character of baptism. The Greek translators, writing for the Jews of the diaspora, urged their readers to see themselves as God's temple opened to the Gentiles. If the translators had in mind a "priestly" service, they did not see it as a cultic function in a closed temple, but as an apostolic service for all mankind.

The author of 1 Peter seems to have adopted this same universalist and missionary vision in his letter to Christians living in their "diaspora." He wants the Christian community to be an open temple and a "body of priests" to "declare the wonderful deed of him who called you out of darkness into his own marvelous light" (1 Pet. 2:9). The Christian "royal residence," therefore, is to perform an apostolic, teaching role toward non-Christians, fulfilling its "spiritual sacrifices" (1 Pet. 2:5) while on the way to unity with all peoples. In other words, Christians have a vital apostolate as translators of the Gospel message to those who persecute and oppose them. This they accomplish by their words and their deeds. As a "body of priests" they are first of all "apostles"; their "priestly" sacrifice is their entire missionary task of gathering all mankind to Christ.

The baptismal vocation as presented in this letter possesses, therefore, a truly historical character. Christians share a common vocation to lead their friends and adversaries to "glorify God on the day of his visitation" (1 Pet. 2:12). All that Christians say and do is to help bring about God's Kingdom of truth, love, and justice in all mankind. The image of the Christian community as a "body of priests" to build up God's "spiritual household" makes eminent sense as a description of the Church's common, yet diversified apostolic mission.

Several points concerning the New Testament images of "mission" and "body of priests" remain to be stated.

1. The Christian community's life of worship is the principal source of nourishment for its active pilgrimage. True proclamation of the Word in cultic sacrifice blends together with Christian action so that worship becomes the sign, symbol, and sacrament of the community's openness to the world. 1 Peter, therefore, does not downplay cultic activity. The community's cultic life, representing a concentration of energies turned completely toward God, serves as the source and the crowning of its dialogic activity with the world.

2. 1 Peter, in advancing the image of a "body of priests," does not refer to the individual baptized person as a priest. Its meaning is collective. First-century Christians, as much as Jews of Old Testament times, would have been reluctant to designate an individual as a "priest." The ancient Israelites accentuated a collective priesthood in their corporate priestly institutions, and first-century Christians placed their emphasis on

the one and unique priesthood of Christ. If we are to maintain fidelity to the original intention of 1 Peter and still recognize its diverse interpretations throughout the history of the Church, certain criteria are needed to understand the collective and individual meanings that the text can provide.

3. These criteria must be sought in returning to Jesus' fundamental intention as found in the New Testament and the most constant currents in ecclesial tradition. Certainly Jesus did not intend to set himself up as a "pontifex maximus," bridging a hierarchical and a common priesthood. What he did was to send committed, dedicated disciples into the world. No one can deny that this "sending forth" came to be structured along the cultic systems of the Old Testament. But the priestly structure of the New Testament makes sense ultimately only by reference to its apostolic structure. The apostolate indicated in texts like Matthew 28:18-20 is the key to understanding the "priesthood of the faithful."

4. The fundamental reality expressed in the images of "temple," "spiritual house," "royal residence" and "body of priests" is, therefore, collective, presuming a convergence of personal faith actions. The "living stones," open-armed and receptive toward society, construct an open and welcoming Church. Christians let their apostolic calling shine forth as they manifest in their actions a Gospel passion for unity, even in the midst of their own diversities and internal conflicts. Baptism, in 1 Peter, is the sacrament of mission, and the Church is a collective "priestly" body sent to build up the Kingdom of God among men.

In our final section we shall examine briefly how the theology of charisms fits into the idea that baptism, by preserving and encouraging temporal and relational bonds, is the sacrament of Christian historicity.

4. Charisms as Related to Baptism

When looking at the concrete conditions in which Christians live out their personal histories, a danger arises in concentrating too much on terms like "apostolate" or "body of priests." Few indeed are the moments or situations that appear directly "apostolic" or "priestly."

Salvation, as we have indicated above, signifies fullness, integrity, and harmony in human existence. How, then, can work be integrated into the life of the baptized to help them achieve fullness and destiny? We can begin to formulate an answer to these questions by looking at St. Paul's theology of charisms.

Paul's ideas are dominated by his emphasis on the common good of the community. In both the Roman and the Corinthian communities, the charisms are gifts of the Spirit called forth and designated by the community's needs. (In this way, it should be noted, needs become an important theological category.) The sick, for instance, need the gift of healing; the indigent, the gift of sharing; community order, the gift of governing and leadership. Each of the charisms—wisdom, learning, prayer, prophecy, together with the charismatic states enjoyed by the apostles and teachers—answers a community need. Of all the charisms, the most durable and constructive, says Paul, is charity, itself an answer to a permanent community need.

From this starting point we can begin to elaborate a theology of work. The first question we need to ask is this: If the charisms help to build up the community and aid the baptized in achieving fullness and integrity in their lives, in what way do they relate to the Christians' natural aptitudes and talents? Are they harmonious with technical and intellectual abilities, or in competition with them?

Charisms, as manifestations of God's grace, build on nature. Taking root in our natural and acquired aptitudes and talents, they give them orientation, directing our specific tasks and vocations to Christ. Normally, then, charisms do not work at cross-purposes with natural gifts; rather, they help realize natural potential. The baptized, therefore, in their natural talents and aptitudes, serve God's plan of fullness and integrity; their work is itself charismatic.

This intimate relationship between the Spirit's charisms and the baptized's natural gifts sets the foundation for the theology of work. Today's Christians live out their pilgrimage toward personal and communal fulfillment largely in their work world. There they seek self-fulfillment and integrity, striving to contribute so that others may also be fulfilled. There also their charisms come to life. Called forth by the tangible needs of society, charisms help the baptized serve justice, freedom, and truth. They represent God's power and concern put into motion in both personal and communal historicity to stir up worn-out hearts and open new doors to individuals and communities too long closed in on themselves.

5. Baptism and Its Political Implications

A concluding word needs to be said on the political

implications flowing from baptism. We have already indicated the sacrament's dialectical character, symboliz-
ing the Christian Church's growth in its struggle toward
fullness and integrity. In this growth process, the
Church has a strongly messianic vocation. Even the
word "Christianity" has a clear etymological reference
to the Messiah, that future, hope-filled political figure
so much a part of the conscience of Israel. Although
Jesus refused to set up a political kingdom, his criticism
of political leaders and of people too submissive to their
oppression certainly possessed political overtones. His
demands for justice, moreover, were not reserved for
his small band of disciples; they were for society as a
whole.

Christians, baptized into Jesus' own history, cannot remain on-lookers to the political conflicts of their
day. They are present to the world's crises to transform
them along a truly dialectical path. Because they carry
as part of their baptismal heritage a relational and temporal historicity that transcends immediate problems,
Christians work to move beyond what is to what can
be. Each of the baptized, as well as the Church as a
whole, is marked by baptism to be socially and poli-
tically critical of society, as yeast in the dough.

Perhaps nothing more characteristically marks the
Christian approach to society's problems than the virtue of hope. Because the baptized look beyond the immediate to the creation of the future, they bring to the
world's agonies a freshness reflecting the New Testament charism of joy. Yet, this hope-sourced joy is
neither foolish nor naive; it springs from constantly
pressing on from the past through the present to create
the future. Counting on God, themselves, and their fel-
low men and women, Christians absorb in their reflec-

tions and actions all the diverse factions they encounter, living them out in tension and in tears, to build up the Kingdom of God under the sign of their risen Lord's cross.

Notes

1. For this section and for what follows, cf. E. Barbotin, *The Humanity of Man*, tr. by Matthew J. O'Connell (Maryknoll, New York: Orbis Books, 1975), 91-136; J-P. Sartre, *Being and Nothingness*, tr. by Hazel E. Barnes (New York: Philosophical Library, 1956), 107-170; M. Merleau-Ponty, *The Phenomenology of Perception*, tr. by Colin Smith (New York: Humanities Press, 1962), 410-433.

2. Cf. E. Mounier, *Personalism*, tr. by Philip Mairet (New York: Grove Press, 1952).

3. Cf. "Marxism," *Sacramentum Mundi* 3 (New York: Herder and Herder, 1969), 419-429.

4. Cf. R. Garaudy, *From Anathema to Dialogue: A Marxist Challenge to the Christian Churches*, tr. by Luke O'Neill (New York: Herder and Herder, 1966).

5. E. Bloch, "Das Prinzip Hoffnung," *Gesamtausgabe*, Bd. V (Frankfurt, 1959).

6. J. Habermas, citing Adorno in *Uber Th. W. Adorno* (Frankfurt/Main: Suhrkamp Verlag, 1968), 40.

7. W. Pannenberg, *What Is Man? Contemporary Anthropology in Theological Perspectives*, tr. by Duane A. Priebe (Philadelphia: Fortress Press, 1970).

8. Cf. H. M. Horkheimer, *Critique of Instrumental Reason*, tr. by Matthew J. O'Connell and others (New York: Seabury Press, 1974).

9. On the "historicizing" influence of Christianity on neo-Hinduism, neo-Buddhism, and neo-Islamism, cf. J. Margull, "Nationalismus und Religion in Asien und Afrika," *RGG* 4, 1316ff. Several works in English are cited in Margull's short bibliography.

10. Cf. J. Coppens, "Mystères paiens et baptême chrétien," *DBS* 1, 903-924; L. Beinart, "Symbolisme mythique de l'eau dans le baptême," *La Maison-Dieu*, 22 (1951), 94-120; J. Cazeneuve, *Les rites et la condition humaine* (Paris, 1958); L. Bouyer, *Rite and Man* (Notre Dame, 1963).

11. Cf. V. Warnach, "Mensch," *Handbuch Theologischer Grudnbegriffe,* II, 145ff. Warnach's bibliography includes several English references.

12. A. Benoit, *Le baptême chrétien au second siècle* (Paris, 1953), 12-27.

13. *Ibid.,* 16.

14. F-M. Braun, "Le Maudeisme et la secte essenienne de Qumran," in *L'Ancien Testament et L'Orient* (Louvain: Publicistes Universitaires, 1957), 193-230.

15. For Paul's baptismal theology, cf. R. Schnackenburg, *Baptism in the Thought of St. Paul,* tr. by G. R. Beasley-Murray (New York: Herder and Herder, 1964).

16. H. Conzelmann, *A Commentary on the First Epistle to the Corinthians,* tr. by J. W. Leitch, bibliography and references by J. W. Dunkly, ed. by G. W. Mac Rae, S.J. (Philadelphia: Fortress Press, 1975).

17. Cf. E. Haulotte, *La symbolique du vêtement selon la Bible* (Paris, 1966), 217-222, 304-309; G. R. Beasley-Murray, *Baptism in the New Testament* (Grand Rapids Mich.: Eerdmans, 1962), 146ff.; R. Schnackenburg, *op. cit.,* 23-26.

18. Cf. J-P. Sartre, *op. cit.,* 361ff.

19. Cf. A. Benoit, *op. cit.*

20. Cf. K. Barth, *Church Dogmatics,* IV/4, tr. by G. W. Bromiley (Edinburgh: T. and T. Clark, 1969).

21. Cf. *In Joan.* 41:11; *Opus imperf. contra Jul.* 5:38.

22. K. Barth, *op. cit.,* 164-194.

23. J. Daniélou, in *La Croix,* April 23, 1971.

24. J-P. Sartre, *The Words,* tr. by Bernard Frechtman (New York: George Braziller, 1964), 99.

25. F. Schmalz, "Kommt es zu einter Revision der Taufpraxis? Uberlegungen in Frankreich und in der Bundesrepublik," *Herder Korrespondenz,* 26. Jhrg./1, Jan. 1972, 14-16.

26. D. Bonhoeffer, *Letters and Papers from Prison,* ed. by Eberhard Bethge (New York: Macmillan, 1967), 210.

27. Cf. W. Kasper, "A New Dogmatic Outlook on the Priestly Ministry," *Concilium* 43, tr. by John Drury (New York: Paulist Press, 1969), 20-33.

28. Cf. K. Rahner, "Anonymous Christians," *Theological Investigations* VI. Translated by Karl and Boniface Kruger (Baltimore: Helicon Press, and London: Darton, Longman, and Todd, 1969), 390-398.

29. Cf. Vatican II, *Decree on Ecumenism*, n. 11.

30. "Catholica et summa illius bonitas" (*Adv. Marc.* 2:17).

31. W. Kasper, *Christsein ohne Enstscheidung* (Mainz: Mathias Grünewald, 1970), 136.

32. Cf. P. Gerbé, "Ils demandent le baptême pour leur enfant," *Parole et Mission* 10 (1966); and "Document épiscopal sur la pastorale du baptême," *"La Maison Dieu* 88 (1966), 43-52, 56.

33. Dictionnaire de Quillet (Paris, 1959), 1799/1. Cf. also the *International Encyclopedia of the Social Sciences*, Vol. 14, art. "Socialization" (New York: Macmillan and the Free Press, 1968), 534-562. Webster's *Third International Dictionary* (1961) gives this definition of socialization: "the process by which a human being beginning at infancy acquires the habits, beliefs, and accumulated knowledge of his society through his education and training for adult status."

34. Cf. K. H. Schelkle, *Discipleship and Priesthood*, tr. by Joseph Disselhorst (New York: Herder and Herder, 1965).

35. Cf. H. Küng, *The Church*, tr. by Ray and Rosaleen Ockenden (New York: Sheed and Ward, 1967), 344-359.

36. *Ibid.*, 373.

37. J. H. Elliot, *The Elect and the Holy: An Exegetical Examination of I Peter II, 4-10* (Leiden: E. J. Brill, 1966).